EMERGE

Breakthrough Into
Your Destiny

EMERGE

Breakthrough Into Your Destiny

CHANCE CESSNA

Emerge: Breakthrough Into Your Destiny

Copyright © 2019. Printed in the USA.

ISBN: 9781791572013

Instagram: www.instagram.com/chancecessna

Facebook: www.facebook.com/iamchancecessna

YouTube: www.youtube.com/user/chancecessna

Twitter: www.twitter.com/chancecessna

Book Cover Photography: Jason McCoy Photography
Book Cover Design: Elle Designs
Book Cover Wardrobe: Stylist and Creative Director of Model Atelier Robin H.

For more information or bulk orders visit:
www.chancecessna.com

DEDICATION

This book is dedicated to every person that seeks to silence every voice of fear, shame, and self-doubt. This book is dedicated to those who desire to awaken the true warrior within. This book is dedicated to those who desire greater depths of focus, clarity, peace, knowledge, wisdom, and joy in pursuit of their life's purpose. To those who have decided they will no longer be held captive by yesterday's setbacks and mistakes. To those who will not be defined by the labels this world has placed on them. To those who want to break out and unleash the raw, authentic, and miraculous power, God has uniquely placed inside of them. To the unstoppable trailblazers, culture shifters, and future history makers of this world, let your light shine. It's time to emerge.

ACKNOWLEDGMENTS

I would like to first thank God, my Heavenly Father, for giving me the vision, wisdom, and strength to finish this book. Without Him, I am nothing. I would like to thank my mother, Cessna Ria Durr, who nurtured and cultivated the most powerful gift that one can ever receive from God - the gift of creativity. I would like to thank my former professor from George Washington University, Steve Roberts, for inspiring me to write without fear or limitation. I would like to thank my friend, publicist Paul Patterson, for being so supportive throughout my journey. I would like to thank my grandmother, Fannie Durr, my sister, Gabrielle Jackson, and my brother, Gabriel Jackson Jr. Lastly, I would like to thank my father, Gabriel Jackson Sr. for being the backbone of our family, and raising us as a single father. I wouldn't have made it this far without all your prayers, love, and support. I love and appreciate you all so much.

emerge - to manifest oneself, arise, materialize, become apparent, spring up, make visible, unfold, and come forth.

CONTENTS

Introduction | Bloom 1

Chapter One | Dear Invisible Me 5

Chapter Two | The Authentic You........................... 21

Chapter Three | The Birthing Process.................... 36

Chapter Four | Fear Traps 48

Chapter Five | Evolving Seasons 64

Chapter Six | Love & Wholeness 74

Chapter Seven | The Blueprint to Success 86

Chapter Eight | The Pit to The Palace 97

Chapter Nine | Emerge Stories................................110

References 121

INTRODUCTION
BLOOM

"You don't have to be great to start, but you have to start to be great."
Zig Ziglar

I held the handles of my seat in a slight sweat. I took a long deep breath and closed my eyes. As my mind began to roam and think about everything that could go wrong, I quietly began to pray under my breath. "Deep breath, Chance. You got this. Don't be afraid. Only believe." As I began to feel the rumbling under my feet, I closed my eyes even more tightly holding on to the cold metal armrest. As we accelerated forward against the wind, I held my breath, and we lifted off into the sky.

This scenario would play out almost every time I boarded a flight, right before the pilot took off on the runway. Preparing for takeoff had always aroused so much anxiety in me and had become my greatest fear while traveling. I would never experience this anxiety once the plane was in the air, or when we were preparing to land. It would only occur when the plane would begin to emerge and ascend into the heavens. It would only happen, when we as the passengers, were about to transition from one dimension to another. It would only occur when we were preparing to shift from the possible, to the impossible.

From a place that felt safe, to the unknown. It would transpire the moment we decided to defy gravity, and no longer allow the ground to hold us captive.

I was born and raised in Chicago, Illinois. My mom was a salon owner, and my dad, a real estate investor. I was raised by my father, who worked 12-16 hour days to create a better life for his family. Long days and even longer nights, my dad did the best he could to provide for us as a single father of three.

When I was just three years old, my mother and father divorced as a result of irreconcilable differences. Many people ask how I got my name Chance. Before the divorce, my parents had briefly split. After some time apart, they decided to get back together and take a second chance at love. I was born and introduced to this world as a result.

I am the youngest of three siblings and have always been my own wildflower. I always had big dreams, possessed many talents, and have been extremely creative. However, I was not always outspoken concerning my talents, skills, and gifts. My dad reminds me all the time that when I was born, I didn't even cry. "She never cried ever" my dad always shares. My father says I was a quiet and precocious child. My uncle even inquired with my grandma, questioning if I was "ok" since he never really heard me talk much.

Growing up, I would have very vivid dreams and visions as a

child that were often hard to explain. Many of those dreams, felt supernatural and futuristic. Not understanding how to articulate them, I would often just keep quiet and journal about them in my diary. The times I would try to express myself at an early age, I often felt that perhaps my voice was not significant enough to be heard or respected as a youth. As a result, I bottled up a lot of my feelings until I became courageous enough to finally start sharing my true thoughts, feelings, and emotions. With time I slowly began to emerge out of my comfort zone, and eventually evolve and flourish into the woman I have become today.

In this book, I not only hope to give you a raw and honest glimpse inside of my life, but also invite you on this journey to emerge into the next level of faith, authenticity, truth, power, healing, love, success, influence, and adventure with me. I will cover the following topics and offer guidance on how to transition from where you are, to where you truly desire to be in life.

Learn How To Emerge From

1. From Fear to Faith
2. From Buried Dreams to Risen Dreams
3. From Hopeless to Hopeful
4. From Hidden to Seen
5. From Stagnancy to Action
6. From Pain to Joy
7. From Shame & Insecurity to Self-Love and Acceptance
8. From Unfulfillment to Fulfillment
9. From Defeat to Victory
10. From Unforgiveness to Forgiveness
11. From Ungratefulness to Gratitude
12. From Worry to Peace
13. From Bondage to Freedom
14. From Lack to Abundance
15. From Brokenness to Wholeness

CHAPTER ONE

DEAR INVISIBLE ME

"Vision is the art of seeing what is invisible to others."
Jonathan Swift

Have you ever walked into a room full of people and felt invisible? With the culmination of all the skills, talents, and gifts uniquely wrapped up inside you, somehow you still remained to walk out and feel unnoticed. Simply put, you felt overlooked. You felt hidden in plain sight.

Every world changer and visionary started at this point. They went days, months, years, and even decades feeling invisible. The one thing that made them different from the average person, however, was that they continued to work when no one was watching. They studied their craft, and they perfected their skills. They created and outlined their vision and continued to execute day after day. They were silently winning battles and defeating giants. They did not grow weary in doing well. They did not give up when people told them to quit. They worked when the stands were empty, and no one was cheering them on. They learned to be consistent in the absence of a public applause.

A couple of years back, I had an appearance on stage in Indiana just a few hours north from my hometown. There were thousands of people anticipating on attending this event. I had been looking forward to this moment for months. There were several acts scheduled on stage that day, but I was determined to be the "stand out" act. I had prepared, worked hard, and felt extremely confident and ready. I thought to myself, "This is finally my moment!" I went on stage and gave it my best shot. It was the best three minutes of my life. Well, at least I thought.

Moments after exiting the stage, however, I was only to be greeted by an insensitive and sarcastic remark by a patron. "You were on stage? I didn't even see you. I was right there in front and had my eyes on the stage the whole time! You couldn't have been up there!" They then chuckled and disappeared into the crowd. Within a moment, all the confidence that I had worked up was crushed. I began to shrink in humiliation and thought to myself, "How could I have possibly been overlooked? How many others had overlooked me? I was right there in the middle of the stage! Was I not good enough? Am I invisible? I had mustered up every ounce of courage to get up there in front of thousands of people, and I walked away feeling defeated. The days following, I began to shrink deeper and deeper into a place of fear, insecurity, and self-pity.

The truth is, we have all been overlooked to some capacity. Whether it was on our jobs, in our careers, at school, in rela-tionships, in our marriages, or in our families. Everyone wants to feel loved, appreciated, valued, and seen. However, that reality for many seems hard to attain.

However, the most important question is this. "Do you see you?"

Did you know that at least 72% of Americans feel lonely, overlooked, and unloved? As a result, this negatively impacts their self-esteem and can damage the perception they have of themselves as people. As this impacts their self-esteem, it can hinder and blur their vision and pursuit of the future. This cycle leads to many people never striving to achieve their highest goals and dreams in life, because they don't feel like they alone are enough.

The first step to emerging into your destiny is "seeing" you and understanding that you alone are enough. It is recognizing the power that truly lies within you and silencing outsiders that make you doubt your potential. It is realizing the fullness of both your beauty and flaws, strengths and weaknesses, and accepting it. Seeing yourself requires you to be present, vulnerable, and honest. Seeing yourself requires you to truly be confident in who you are, despite what you have been through. It is fully understanding that when God, the Creator of the universe made you, He formed you in your mother's womb and fashioned you to perfection. It is understanding that you are first His workmanship, His ultimate design, and His most magnificent masterpiece. It is understanding how powerful you truly are.

"God created mankind in his own image, in the image of God he created them; male and female." Genesis 1:27 (NIV)

Do you know that you are made in the image of God? Do you know you are handcrafted by the Creator of the universe Himself? From your ethnicity, skin color, hair texture, height, and looks, God uniquely and strategically designed you with great love and intention. The same One who created the stars in the sky, and put the moon and sun in its place, is the same One who created you.

Did you know that God even knows the exact count of hairs on your head? Luke 12:7 (NLT) says, "The very hairs on your head are all numbered." He's completely in tune with every detail of your life and knows you intimately. Before you were formed in your mother's womb, God knew you, set you apart, and created you for a purpose. Before you were even a thought in your parent's mind, God had a plan for your life. Your life is not an accident.

To emerge, you must first do an honest evaluation of how you see yourself. How you see yourself, directly correlates to how you see the world, and how you plan for the future. Your perception of yourself has influenced every decision you have made in this life up until this very moment. From jobs you have worked, to the people you have dated, to the friends you have chosen, to the neighborhood you live in, to the life you have built for yourself, your current reality is the total summation of all the decisions you have made up until this point. All the decisions you have made up until now, have been solely built upon the foundation of how you see yourself. Do you believe in yourself? Do you value and respect yourself? What defines your self-worth? Do you like the person you have become? Do you love yourself?

When you don't sincerely acknowledge, love, and accept yourself first, it's a recipe for what I call the "invisible state." In this state, you begin to count yourself out, and start counting everyone else in. You prematurely disqualify yourself because you compare your life to others and listen to the opinions of those who have no power concerning your destiny. You take yourself out of the game, before you even get a true chance to play on the court. When you evaluate how you see yourself, it brings light to the areas of your life that have been neglected, and allows you to make the necessary adjustments.

It's not until you learn how to value, love, and respect yourself, that you will be able to value, love, and respect others to the fullest measure and highest capacity.

What kind of relationship do you have with yourself? What would the "invisible" you say? What kind of relationship do you have with God? What do your relationships look like with other people? Assessing these three areas is vital to your success.

What Is Love?

"Love is patient, love is kind. It does not envy, it does not boast, it is not proud. It does not dishonor others, it is not self-seeking, it is not easily angered, it keeps no records of wrongs."
1 Corinthians 13:4-5 (NIV)

True love empowers and revives the human soul. True love heals. True love arrests fear and elevates confidence. True love inspires creativity and ignites vision. It's God's love for us, that first gives us the power to love ourselves. John 3:16 (NIV) states, "For God so loved the world, that he gave his only begotten Son [Jesus], that whosoever believeth in him should not perish, but have everlasting life." We are to love God because He first loved us and made the ultimate sacrifice to prove it.

The Greatest Commandment

Jesus declared, "'Love the Lord your God with all your heart and with all your soul and with all your mind. This is the first and greatest commandment. And the second is like it: 'Love your neighbor as yourself. All the Law and the Prophets hang on these two commandments." Matthew 22:37-40 (NIV)

Without understanding God's love for us, and how we were designed to love Him back, we can never love ourselves fully and properly. We can neither love others properly. The Scripture tells us to love our neighbor as we love ourselves, so the act of love first begins with us. God's lavish love sets the standard of love on every level. I realized when I performed on stage that day in Indiana, I didn't truly love and believe in myself. Even though I told myself I did, I would often allow other people's opinions to shatter my confidence. Regardless of that person's remark, if I truly believed in myself, I would have walked off stage feeling confident that day, knowing that I did the best I could do. I would have held my head high, knowing I worked hard to get there, and whether I was approved in public or not, that I had already been approved in private by God.

"It is not that we think we are qualified to do anything on our own. Our qualification comes from God."
2 Corinthians 3:5 (NLT)

The moment you realize that your value comes from God your Creator and not people, there is a rare and fresh boldness that will empower you. It's God's love that qualifies and validates us, not titles, positions, people, relationships, past setbacks, or mistakes. God's love affirms us and equips us for our next level. That shift in your understanding will begin to redefine and reshape your entire outlook on life. It has the power to reshape how you used to see yourself, and give you a new vision and a fresh perspective of the future. The moment you realize and embrace the fact you are extremely loved and were created by God to fulfill a specific purpose, the moment you understand that everything you have been through was not in vain, that's when your true self begins to take the first significant step towards emerging into your true power.

There was once a woman named Hannah in the Bible. For many years, she cried out to God to open her womb and give her a child. She had been barren for many years. She was mocked and ridiculed, often by the people closest to her. For years, Hannah was bullied and shamed. She experienced the "invisible state."

It seemed that for years, she was being overlooked and everyone was moving ahead of her. The scripture says, "She wept and would not eat" 1 Samuel 1:7 (NIV). In today's terms, this woman was deeply depressed.

Although she was in a place of deep sorrow and despair, instead of becoming bitter and angry, she was honest and vulnerable, and cried out to God.

"And she made a vow, saying, "Lord Almighty, if you will only look on your servant's misery and remember me, and not forget your servant but give her a son, then I will give him to the Lord all the days of his life." 1 Samuel 1:11 (NIV)

Upon remaining steadfast in hope, prayer, and faith, God had answered Hannah's prayer. Shortly after, Hannah conceived and gave birth to a son. She dedicated him to God and named him Samuel. Her son eventually went on to become one of the most powerful and respected prophets and leaders of all time.

Hannah's cry to be seen by God was heard. Hannah's unwavering faith birthed her dream. She perceived that there was a seed of greatness on the inside of her that had to be birthed, although for many years there was no physical evidence. She was barren. Yet, there was something on the inside of her that knew, this is not the way my story is supposed to end. She didn't allow how she once saw herself, to impact the version of herself she wanted to emerge into. She emerged despite how people saw her on the outside, and despite how she may have privately saw herself at times.

It was her boldness, and ability to come out of the shadows of shame and self-pity, and into the light of knowing she had the power to be seen and heard by God, that exalted her.

In Hannah's fight, she emerged into her destiny. As a result, she went from feeling invisible, to becoming highly sought-after and respected. She went from being shamed in the public eye, to fame in the public eye. God promoted her from the background to the foreground. God favored Hannah, and she went on to give birth to several other children. Now, she has become one of the most inspirational women of the Bible and is still inspiring lives until this day. Hannah went from shame to fame. This is one example of moving from the invisible to visible.

Do you believe that God can take you from shame to fame? Do you believe that He can exchange your ashes for beauty? Do you believe that God can take you from a place of feeling overlooked and forgotten, to being fully loved, seen, appreciated, and celebrated for who you authentically are?

> "The purpose in a man's heart is like deep water, but
> a man of understanding will draw it out."
> Proverbs 20:5 (ESV)

Just as a person goes to a well to draw out water, purpose must be drawn out of you. It is a deliberate and intentional pursuit to reveal and uncover what already lives in the treasure chest of your soul. Pursuing purpose demands you to draw deeper and expand into the unknown. It summons you to shatter the invisible ceiling you have been living under for far too long.

Hannah did not let other people's opinions distract or deter her from her dream to have children and leave a legacy. Like a well, she continued to draw until she got the results her heart desired. She continued to fight when the odds were against her. Hannah emerged into her destiny as a result of her desire to never give up. She overcame shame, depression, and defeat and had unshakable faith. Your purpose and calling in life should not be abandoned because you don't currently see the outcome. Your pursuit of the future should not be hindered by the fact that it seems impossible. With God, all things are possible.

Emerging requires you to unapologetically break outside of your comfort zone. It demands you to boldly embrace the most authentic version of yourself. It's not until you turn up the volume on who God made you to be, that you will breakthrough into your destiny. It's not until you fully and wholeheartedly believe in yourself and take the limits off your life, that you will experience true freedom. It's not until you come out of hiding, and no longer be afraid of being seen in your moments of both strength and vulnerability, that you will collide with destiny. It's not until you stop seeing everyone else as more qualified or capable than you, that you will emerge beyond your wildest dreams.

You are worthy. You are special. You are beautiful. You are different. You are loved. You are capable. You are gifted. You are talented. You are enough. You must believe this from the very core of your soul. You are more qualified than you think, and you must believe that you are worthy of living the life you have always dreamed.

How much further would you be in life, if you silenced every voice that contradicted and attempted to derail your ultimate career and life ambitions? How much further would you be if you stopped trying to please people and live within their confines of what they thought your success should look like? How would you emerge if you evicted every fear, doubt, and insecurity that tried to invade your "promised land" of success?

Signs of the "Invisible State"

1.) You hide behind your fears and insecurities, and list excuses why you have not started the project, plan, or business when you know you should have started already.

2.) You often overlook your own passions and desires, and regularly deem others as more qualified than you, even when they may not be.

3.) You do not invest in yourself on a consistent basis.

4.) You often feel unworthy.

5.) Overall, you spend more time investing in other people and other things, than focusing on the bigger picture of what you actually want out of life. You label it as putting others "first" which we all should very well do. Yet often, it's really just a cover up to take the responsibility and focus off you. You intentionally pursue distractions to pull focus from yourself.

These following practical steps are the very steps that can change your life and accelerate and position you to emerge.

1.) Love is the Cure

When the world turns its back against you, know that God's love never fails and is everlasting toward you. Allow God's love to be your power supply, lifeline, and support system. Let His

---

love and guidance be the fuel for your passions and pursuits. God has given us one life. Value your life, take care of your life, and manage your life well. The better you love yourself based on the understanding of God's love for you, the more confident you will become. As a result, you will be better able to love, give, help, and serve others.

2.) Invest in Yourself

Invest in yourself every day and in every way possible. You can't pour from an empty cup. Invest in yourself physically, spiritually, mentally, and emotionally. Just like a bank, the more you deposit into yourself, the more valuable you will be come to others. You will become more valuable to those on your job, those at your church, those in your community, and ultimately, the world around you.

If you are reading this and thinking about going back to school, go back. If you are thinking about starting that non-profit or business, find mentors in your field and sit under them to teach you.

The more deposits you begin to make within yourself, the more you will begin to see your credibility and self-esteem increase. You will become a better asset to your family, community, and the world at large.

An investment in yourself, pays the best interest.

3.) Stop People Pleasing

You can't please everyone and carry out your purpose at the same time.

On your journey, people will disagree with you, and some will even hate and despise you. Sorry to break the news to you, but you will never make everyone happy. Keep God first, let Him guide you, and keep going.

4.) Resurrect Your Dreams

What dreams have you buried? Allow yourself to dream again no matter what current predicament you may find yourself in. Activate your imagination and use it to aid your vision as you plan for the future. For three years of my life, I attempted to bury my desire to continue my career in media and entertainment. I would convince myself that I should just move on. Being a storyteller, whether in front of the camera or behind the camera, has always been my lifelong passion. Today, I am pursuing my dreams and God continues to open many doors. What if I kept telling myself, "Just move on, Chance!" I might not have been anywhere near where I am today.

Guard and protect your passions, interests, and career ambitions. Don't talk yourself out of your dream to accommodate your current circumstance. Keep the dream alive and do not let anyone discourage you.

5.) Dismiss Distractions

To emerge, you must be a master at conquering distractions. Decrease the time you spend on social media, delete old phone numbers of people that disrupt your focus, apply for a new job with a better environment, move to a new neighborhood, do whatever it is you have to do to eliminate distractions. The road to success is not easy. You are going to have to learn to navigate the pitfalls distractions often bring. Keep your head in the game, and eyes on the prize.

Reflections

Seeing yourself, and realizing your power and potential, should be your number one priority in this season. It's not selfish to put yourself first, it's wisdom. If you don't love and take care of you first, you will never be able to love and take care of others in a honest, healthy, and consistent way.

You must believe in yourself without wavering and doubting. You can no longer be afraid. You must be brave enough to come from behind the veil and be seen. It's time to turn up the volume on who you truly are. Take a moment to answer the following questions in your journal.

1. How would you describe yourself?
2. How would other people describe you?
3. What areas in your life do you currently feel overlooked or undervalued?
4. What areas of your life do you need to spend more time and energy investing in?
5. What areas of your life have you allowed other people's opinions to hold you back?

CHAPTER TWO

THE AUTHENTIC YOU

"As in water face reflects face, so a man's heart reveals the man."
Proverbs 27:19 (NKJV)

The truth is, sometimes I'm afraid. Sometimes it's hard to trust God. Sometimes I make mistakes. Sometimes I feel like giving up. Sometimes I cry at night because this journey called life feels unbearable. Sometimes I feel terrified and lonely in this big crazy world.

The real me does not like washing and folding clothes. The real me often spends a little too much time on social media and Instagram. The real me regrets dating some of the people I dated in the past. The real me wishes that my parents never divorced in hopes of growing up in a happy and loving home. The real me wishes I never had to face and deal with the shame of my past, based on the poor decisions I made.

What about you? What truths would the authentic you reveal about you?

Many of us are not as aloof and naive as we sometimes portray ourselves to be concerning our current reality. We know the parts of ourselves that we don't like. We know the parts of us that need transformation and healing. We know the areas where we are truly weak, but too afraid to look in the mirror, because our pride blinds and arrest us from doing so.

Looking in the mirror at who you truly are can be difficult. You see the things that you like, and the things you don't like. It's also one of the most liberating and powerful things a person can do. Once you can truly face yourself, you can fearlessly and confidently stand in your own power, and face anything in life.

One night I had a dream. In this dream, it was thousands of people traveling through a busy street intersection. It looked similar to Times Square in New York. I had an aerial view above the crowd. As I looked down and examined the crowd closely, I realized there were people in black hoodies trying to disguise themselves amongst the people. I pondered to myself "What could that mean?"

Suddenly, I found myself walking through that same intersection and I had on the same black hoodie. Out of nowhere, I hear a voice echo through the earth and say, "Reveal yourself!" Chills went down my spine. I knew immediately, it was the voice of God speaking.

In unison, we all began to remove our hoodies and unveil ourselves. You see, we had all been trying to fit into the crowd, pretending to be something we weren't. This was the moment God was calling our true selves to come forth. When everyone's hood came off, we began to manifest our true light and power. And all the world was there to witness and watch. We had emerged into the very power, we had been seeking to hide our entire lives.

In the same way, many of us have been masking our true selves. And God is saying, "Come out of hiding." That dream was not just about me. It was for everyone who knows they have not been living up to their full potential and knows that God is calling them to more. I'm here to tell you. Stop hiding.

"For the creation awaits in eager expectation for the children of God to be revealed." Romans 8:19 (CEV)

All of creation, is anxiously waiting for you to step into your purpose. The world is eagerly waiting on you to follow the call of destiny. Will you respond?

Growing up, I attended church with my family. I always believed that God was real. However, I never went the extra mile outside of church to really learn who God was. In church, they would read the Bible. I would listen, however, I would often try and tune it out. I knew I had done many things in my past that I was ashamed of. I wasn't ready to know God deeper. Deep down, however, I knew that God was calling me to more.

The summer of 2011 marked a dramatic shift in my life. I had recently suffered a loss in the family, just experienced a heartbreak from the guy I thought was the "man of my dreams", and my world seemed like it was crashing down.

June 19th, 2011, I made a decision. Outside of the pressure and influences of those around me, I decided to surrender and give my life wholeheartedly to Jesus Christ. At this time, I had found myself feeling lost, stressed, tired, and broken. I had come to the end of myself. I began to read the Bible, and for the first time ever, it actually made sense to me. I was awakened to the truth and reality of God's Word. My entire life started to begin to make sense. Like a puzzle, God began to show me the pieces of my destiny, and how He was going to make my life perfectly fit together in a way I could never.

I spent that entire summer in pursuit of God. It was incredible. God began to give me a glimpse of my purpose and what I was called to do in this world. God began to heal the broken parts of me and use them to establish me for His purpose. He began to show me that my past and life was not a mistake. He began to show me that He was going to use all my ashes and all of my pain for His glory. God began to show me that the only way to fulfill my real purpose and destiny was through Him, not apart from Him.

Since 2011, my life has never been the same. Making that

decision to surrender and give my life to Christ, was the best decision I have ever made in life.

Emerging requires you to be transparent when it comes to your weaknesses and vulnerabilities. It necessitates you sharing the most delicate parts of yourself with your Creator - God.

To emerge, you must surrender.

"I am the vine; you are the branches. If you remain in Me and I in you, you will bear much fruit; apart from Me you can do nothing." John 15:5 (NKJV)

When you choose God first, you will always be on the winning side. When you develop a personal relationship with Him and nurture that relationship, you will always thrive because He is the vine of life. God will give you strength and nourishment for your journey. He will complete you with every resource you need to win the victory.

When God is backing you, you will prosper in everything you touch. Psalm 112:3 (CSB) says, "Wealth and riches are in His house, and His righteousness endures forever." When you abide in God, you will be rich in every way because true wealth starts from the inside out. It is God's will for you to prosper and succeed. It is His will for you to thrive in your spirituality, health, finances, marriage, family life, and career.

1 Samuel 18:14 (NLT) says, "David continued to succeed in everything he did, for the Lord was with him." When you allow God to guide you, He will give you the greatest strategies for winning on every level. Like David, you will succeed in everything you do. Prayer and meditating on God's Word is the greatest way to develop intimacy with God and learn His heart. It is also the greatest way to understand your purpose and discover precisely what He put you on this earth to do.

Outer Shell vs. Inner Core

Every day, you are faced with the reality of two different versions of yourself. On one hand, you have the outer shell. Your outer shell represents everything you want people to perceive about you, and what people think they know about your life. Your outer shell also represents your current job or career, what kind of car you currently drive, where you live, etc. It is everything people see on the outside. It's a temporary reality that's constantly evolving and changing. Your inner core, however, represents your truest and most authentic desires, aspirations, and dreams. It's what lives in the seat of your soul. It is your deepest yearnings in life. Your inner core is who you truly are.

Unlike the outer shell, your inner core does not change. The whispers of your inner core are always consistent and always speaking, no matter how long you have tried to suppress it.

Many of us spend our lives attempting to attain things outside of ourselves, not realizing that everything that you are seeking in life, is already within you. With this in mind, the goal should be to break through your outer shell and allow your inner core to manifest and emerge beyond its previous limitations.

Truth and Transparency

Living a life of transparency and honesty will bring you into a level of freedom many have yet to experience. Living life when no one has the potential to blackmail you from things you did in your past, is the most liberating feeling ever.

Growing up, like most teenagers, I would occasionally sneak out of the house, and not get permission from my parents to do certain things. However, when I would do this, I would always be paranoid that I was going to get caught. There is no worse feeling than being afraid you are going to get caught!

When you live and walk in truth however, you have nothing to hide. Even when people try to plot against you, their plans will not prevail because truth is greater than a lie.

"Then you will know the truth, and the truth will set you free."
John 8:32 (NIV)

Imagine living a life totally free. Imagine being free from all your fears and walking in perfect love and trust. Imagine walking in true freedom, despite past accusations people tried to pin against you. Imagine living life guilt-free. The beautiful thing that I love about God, is the fact that once we sincerely come to Him, and repent about our past wrongdoings, He forgives us and wipes our slate clean!

> "Come now, let us settle the matter," says the LORD. "Though your sins are like scarlet, they shall be as white as snow; though they are red as crimson, they shall be like wool."
> Isaiah 1:18 (NIV)

What the enemy will try to do is convince you that your past failures, mistakes, and shortcomings, are still being held against you to keep you from emerging and breaking through into victory. The enemy will use people's past to torment them and make them fearful about the future. The enemy wants to keep you stuck and stagnant, while Jesus has come to bring freedom, and liberate you from every form of bondage and fear.

> "It is for freedom that Christ has set us free. Stand firm, then, and do not let yourselves be burdened again by a yoke of slavery." Galatians 5:1 (NIV)

God sent His son Jesus to be given as a ransom for all of humanity. Jesus took the penalty we all deserved as sinners. He was brutally crucified on the Cross over 2,000 years ago so we can be saved, have authority over the enemy, and have access to the free gift of eternal life through Him. The punishment we deserved because of our sin, Jesus was the one to stand in our place.

> "He died for everyone so that those who receive his new life
> will no longer live for themselves. Instead they will live for
> Christ, who died and was raised for them. "
> 2 Corinthians 5:15 (NLT)

Jesus sacrificed His life so that we can experience the abundant life. He did this so we could conquer every enemy and adversary to our destiny. He did this to give us power over fear, depression, shame, sickness, and defeat.

Simply put, sin separates us from God. Sin makes you break laws that were meant to keep you safe and protect your soul. Sin displaces us outside of His perfect will. Sin has the power to interrupt and hinder your progress and keep you from emerging.

Sin is not your friend. It's your enemy. With Jesus, however, you can acquire the power to overcome everything that would aim to keep you in bondage.

Romans 10:9 (NIV) says, "If you declare with your mouth, "Jesus is Lord," and believe in your heart that God raised him from the dead, you will be saved." Faith begins where man's power ends. When you confess and put your faith in Jesus, He will give you the power to do all things. You will be unstoppable. All you have to do is declare and believe.

What's In Your Garden?

"I am the true vine, and My Father is the keeper of
the vineyard. He cuts off every branch in Me that
bears no fruit, and every branch that does bear fruit,
He prunes to make it even more fruitful."
John 15:2 (BSB)

Imagine a garden. If it were wild and untamed, who would want to eat of the fruit of that garden? If the garden, however, was beautiful, well nurtured and maintained, who would not want to eat fruit from that garden?

Gardening can take a lot of hard work, time, sweat, and energy. Gardening maintenance requires preparing your soil, planting your crops, and nurturing and giving your garden the care and attention it needs. It takes patience and diligence.

There's one thing you must look out for however that can be detrimental to the growth and success of your garden. Weeds. Weeds can be defined as "plants out of place." They compete with garden plants for water and nutrients, and harbor insects and diseased pests. Weeds keep life from emerging in your garden. They disguise themselves as flowers, only to attack and hinder the growth of real plants. Eliminating weed growth as early as possible is the key to a successful, flourishing, and budding garden.

Now consider your life as a garden. What kind of flowers have blossomed from the garden of your life? What kind of weeds have sprouted up in your garden? What kind of seeds are planted in the soil of your heart? Are there seeds of bitterness? Fear? Anger? Jealousy? Gossip? Slander? Impatience? Pride? Unforgiveness? Examining yourself and knowing what's in you is critical to your growth and success.

It is our responsibility to be the caretakers of the garden of our lives. It is our responsibility to work toward pulling up the necessary weeds that are crippling our growth, and that are fatal to our destiny.

"Catch for us the foxes, the little foxes that ruin the vineyards, our vineyards that are in bloom." Song of Solomon 2:15 (NIV)

Don't let the little foxes keep you from advancing and experiencing the full measure of blessings God has for you. Similar to weeds, little foxes hinder your progress, and keep you from seeing the full harvest of your destiny. Little foxes are things that appear small in the beginning, but are deadly, poisonous, and dangerous in the end. Watch out for these traps.

We must be aggressive about removing threats from the garden that represents our lives. The sooner you identify them, the greater the harvest you will see in the end.

There was once a woman named Amy. She had a beautiful garden filled with all types of rare fruits and vegetables. One summer, a severe drought occurred in California. In a typical year, California gets no rain from about May-October. Not a drop. That's just regular California weather without considering the effects of climate change.

During the time of this drought, Amy and many others began hiring a lawn painting service to paint their dead grass green. It became extremely popular around town. This began to make me think about people's lives. How many of us have suffered a drought in our own lives? This picture portrays what a lot of us do. We paint the garden of our life to make it appear healthy and prosperous while underneath, it's dead. We mask who and what we truly are.

Most of us are guilty of caring more about what things look like on the outside, rather than what they actually look like on the inside. As I began to analyze my garden, there were and still are many areas in my life that need work. However, I am committed to growth. I am committed to evolving and emerging into the woman I desire to become. I know that I am still a work in progress. We all are. When we are honest about who we really are, that's when growth can truly take place. When our hearts and motives are pure, that's when God can begin to do the real work. We will no longer have to hide what's truly underneath.

When our hearts are pure, we can experience God in His fullness and all the incredible things He has for us. When our hearts are pure, and we live a life of transparency, we can experience a greater measure of joy and peace. Psalm 26:2 (KJV) says, "Examine me, O LORD, and try me, examine my heart and my mind." We must be intentional about putting our hearts before God for His careful examination, so He can pull up and uproot things in our lives as He deems necessary.

The Corridors of The Mind

One early morning, I was getting ready to catch a flight at the airport. I packed my bags as usual and was all set to go. I went through the TSA and forgot I had some liquids in my carry on. I was stopped at the security checkpoint. I almost missed my flight because I was delayed an extra ten minutes. It seemed as if it took forever for them to check my bags! It wasn't until all the belongings I had were thoroughly searched, that I could move forward. I got to my airport terminal seconds before they were about to close the door and take off.

The same way TSA searches people at the airport for the safety and protection of travelers, is the same way we need to guard and protect our minds and the thoughts that come into them. You must thoroughly search every negative and self-defeating thought that tries to invade your mind and heart. You can't control every thought that comes to your mind, but you have the power to let those thoughts stay or command them to leave. You have the authority to either block those thoughts out, or give them access in. That day at the airport, I was blocked from entering because my belongings didn't match the criteria. In the same way, we must qualify every thought that attempts to enter our conscious and deter us from destiny.

Your mind is the control center of your life. The average person has 30,000 thoughts a day. You have the power to act on those thoughts or ignore them. Take charge of your thought life. Train yourself to better govern what you allow in your mind, and what you meditate on. Discipline yourself to better manage what you allow in your heart. Protect the garden of your life.

Reflections

It's time to discover the authentic you. Below are some questions that will help guide you.

1) How would you describe the garden of your life?
2) How honest would you say you are with yourself and other people?
3) What areas of your life have you neglected and overlooked that need to be cultivated?
4) How well do you move beyond negative thoughts?

CHAPTER THREE
THE BIRTHING PROCESS

"As a man sows, shall he reap. And all I know is talk is cheap."
Unknown

How many people do you know, speak of things they want to accomplish or become, yet never actually take the necessary steps and action to manifest it? In other words, this person is all talk. We live in a world today where people want instant results and gratification. It is much easier to talk about success, than actually accomplish it. Many people think that success happens by luck or happenstance, yet that could not be any further from the truth.

In the very first book of the Bible, Genesis, the blueprint and formula for the successful birthing of a new life, idea, business, or concept is outlined. Everything that has ever been or ever will be created, must go through this process. Genesis is derived from the Greek word meaning "origin," "source," or the "beginning." When we understand God's "Genesis Strategy," we can begin to identify and break past the barriers that have held us back from giving birth to destiny.

"In the beginning, God created the heavens and the earth. Now the earth was formless and empty, darkness was over the surface of the deep, and the Spirit of God was hovering over the waters." Genesis 1:1-2 (NIV)

When God first created the world, He began creating in the dark. The earth had no shape, no form, and no definition. The only thing that dwelled in the presence of darkness was His Spirit. The earth began with a vision in the mind of God, but it would be a process to see it unfold.

Did you know that every new beginning starts in the dark?

Similar to the creation of the world, the beginning stage of anything new will always be void of form, definition, and complete understanding. When you begin a new chapter or season of your life, and you don't understand or feel alone, it can possibly be because you are in the midst of the most incredible birthing experience you have yet to witness.

Amid the darkness or unknown, the Scripture states that the Spirit of God was "hovering over the waters." God was present, even in the absence of light. In the same manner, since the beginning of your life, God was watching over you. He was present, even when you thought He wasn't there.

From your entry into the earth through your mother's womb, to the day you graduated from grade school, to that day you started that new job, moved to that new city, started that new relationship; God was there. At the beginning of every fresh start in life, God is with us. Understanding this principle and truth is foundational for your success.

When people don't understand the birthing process of destiny, they often abort their purpose. Out of ignorance, they miss out on destiny either because of fear, or their inability to exercise enough patience to watch the vision unfold. When people don't see results instantly, many quit prematurely. Yet, I have learned not to be afraid of the dark, because it's out of darkness, that all great things are born. Without darkness, you will never appreciate the light.

God's Development Strategy for Creation

Day 1: Night and Day
Day 2: Sky and Sea
Day 3: Land and Vegetation
Day 4: Stars, Sun, and Moon
Day 5: Sea Creatures and Birds
Day 6: Animals and Mankind
Day 7: God's Day of Rest

God had a blueprint for success, and because we are made in His image, we should have one too. With each new day, God began to speak and give His creation color, design, structure, and framework. Each day, He carefully built upon His previous days' work. Each day had its own process and construction blueprint. The earth was not fully developed until the sixth day.

It was not until the seventh day, that God rested. He did not stop building until He completed the vision He had for each day. God took His time to construct each element with precision, beauty, and excellence. He never lost focus and never became distracted. Similar to our human experience, when God calls us to birth something new in life, and we are a 100% focused and without distraction, the extraordinary happens. We create the most beautiful, meaningful, purposeful, ideas, designs, products, businesses, and creations. As a result of God having a vision for the world and executing it, all of creation now has a home. God was not building without a purpose or cause. He was building for the beautiful reward that was to come – us, His creation.

Patience is power. In order to successfully give birth to anything new, you must mature in patience. Giving birth requires your full attention to detail, it requires your undivided focus, and most importantly, it requires your patience and faith.

Patience cannot be exercised without faith.

The Scripture defines faith as "Now faith is the reality of what is hoped for, the proof of what is not seen." Hebrews 11:1 (CSB) Faith is a down payment for the future. Faith is seeing in the dark, what has yet to be revealed in the light for others to see. Without faith, we will often quit while God is still developing us. Many of us will be so close to the finish line and give up right before we meet the mark. This is why trusting God's plan for your life is so important.

In every new beginning of your life, in every new season, with every new chapter, with every new endeavor, know that God is with you every step of the way. He created you for an extraordinary purpose and loved you enough to create an entire universe for you to thrive, succeed, and fulfill your purpose in. In moments you feel alone, isolated, overlooked, and forgotten, God is always with you and advocating for your success. Don't rush your process and don't compare your journey to other people's. Your journey should be unique to you and only you. God's process of creating the world was an experience unique to Him and Him alone. We, as His creation just reaped the marvelous benefits.

So patiently build your life day-by-day, chapter-by-chapter, no matter how long it takes. God's process for earth's creation was six days. Yours may be six weeks, six months, or even six years. However, regardless of the time frame, stay the course. Let the work you do today, combined with your faith, be a down payment for your tomorrow.

The Spirit of a Finisher

Growing up, I barely finished anything. I barely finished my homework at times, I barely finished washing the dishes, I barely finished cleaning my room, and the list goes on. I never honestly finished anything to its absolute completion. Unfortunately, I took this habit into my teens and young adult life.

Most of the things I did were half done. I knew the areas where I was secretly being lazy and cutting corners. I knew the areas of my life where I tried looking for a shortcut, did not give my best, and did not complete the task or assignment with excellence.

It's easy to start something. Yet finishing and seeing it through until the end, is an entirely different story. The distance between the idea and achieving the results are often quite vast. For example, according to Bloomberg, 8 out of 10 new businesses fail within the first 18 months. Many companies struggle to get through their first year of operation and usually don't survive.

Beyond starting a business, starting anything new will never be easy, and is not for the faint at heart. Whether it be a new career, a new idea, or a new project, the likelihood of not finishing is high. Why? Because people often by nature, take the path of least resistance. They take this path because quite frankly, it's easier. To emerge however, we must live a life that embraces challenges. We must be committed to finishing what we start.

Emerging is not about doing what's easy. It's about doing what's necessary.

It will be hard, it will be challenging, there will be times you want to quit, but the reward is so much greater in the end. You must have the spirit of a finisher.

Many of us had dreams when we were a child. Yet over time, we buried those dreams and gave up on them. Maybe you figured if you lived a "traditional" life, followed the path of simply working a good job, making average pay, and doing the best you could do, that life would hopefully one day turn out good for you. However, success does not just fall in your lap. You have to work for it, you have to pray for it, and you have to fight for it.

"There is a way that seems right to a man, but its end is the way to death." Proverbs 14:12 (ESV)

What if we applied this Scripture to your path to success? Just because you are traveling in a way that "seems right" in your life, and feels comfortable, does not mean it is the best path. Destiny and comfort can't exist in the same place. Walking in a way that seems right in our eyes can lead to destruction. In this scenario, it can lead to the destruction of our vision, dreams, goals, and destiny. You must be willing to travel a different route. You must be willing to separate from the crowd and go in the direction that God is leading you in. You can no longer be afraid to go against what's popular. Embrace challenges and embrace change.

"After this, Jesus, knowing that all things were now accomplished, that the Scripture might be fulfilled, said, "I thirst!" Now a vessel full of sour wine was sitting there; and they filled a sponge with sour wine, put it on hyssop, and put it to His mouth. So, when Jesus had received the sour wine, He said, "It is finished!" And bowing His head, He gave up His spirit." John 19:28-30 (NKJV)

Jesus is the perfect example of what it looks like to have the spirit of a finisher. By the time He was crucified, He had given this world all He had. Every ounce of power and purpose was poured out like an offering during His time on earth. He died empty and did not quit prematurely. He could not give up His Spirit until He accomplished everything He was supposed to do. At the very end of His experience on earth, He exclaimed, "It is finished!" It was through His finishing work that all of mankind could be redeemed from sin and live the abundant life we all deserve.

There were thousands of generations and billions of people attached to Jesus' determination to finish. You must finish. You must birth the dream, start the business, write the book, produce the movie, or do whatever it is you feel called to do. Whatever the call is you hear ringing in your spirit, answer it. There is an assignment on your life that only you can fulfill. There is a problem in this world, only you can answer. Don't allow your vision to waste away. There are people counting on you to emerge into who God has called you to be. This world needs you to finish.

The Steps of a Finisher

1.) Research

Many people start new projects or implement new ideas without doing proper research. This is a disaster waiting to happen. Never begin a blind work without a vision that has been previously researched and outlined. Educate yourself and become as well informed as you can before taking action on a new pursuit. Count the cost of all the work you will have to put in and set realistic goals.

2.) Build a Solid Foundation

Building a solid foundation requires building on the previous step - research. The more you learn ahead of time, the more pitfalls you can avoid later. Create a vision portfolio, create a solid business plan, and work from that blueprint.

3.) Produce

Start producing real results. Don't overthink it. Get creative and just start. Focus on what's real, and create and produce more of that.

4.) Don't Be Discouraged by Other People's Journey

In the process of birthing something new, you will meet others that have pursued the same thing you want to pursue or something similar. However, don't let their "horror stories" keep you from moving forward. Remember that your journey is unique to you. Just because they failed, quit, or have had mediocre results, that does not have to be your story.

If their project, business, or endeavor is not thriving, that does not mean yours won't. Focus and commit yourself to being diligent day-by-day. Set your mind on good examples to follow and continue to remain in a state of constant creativity, expression, inspiration, and gratitude.

5.) Be Committed To Developing Your Skill Set

Focus on mastering your skill set. Even if you are an expert already, keep seeking to improve. Always continue to learn, develop, and sharpen your abilities. Journal and write down everything you learn along the way and measure your progress.

6.) Discover the Beauty in Patience

Proverbs 21:5 (NASB) says, "The plans of the diligent lead surely to advantage, but everyone who is hasty comes surely to poverty." I have regretted many decisions in the past because I moved too fast. Do nothing in a hurry. People can wait. The world can wait. Commit to doing it right and with excellence. Patience is your greatest asset when it comes to pursuing your purpose. Embrace it and walk in it.

7.) Don't Wait For Others to Celebrate You

Learn to celebrate yourself. Whether small or big, celebrating your achievements is vital. Celebrating yourself reinforces and affirms you with the confidence to continue building for the future. Start taking the time out to do little things to reward yourself along your journey. You're worth it.

Reflections

It's your birthing season. Get ready to create, produce, and get to work! Take a moment and answer the questions below.

1) What have you started that you need to finish in this season of your life?
2) What would you be pursuing if money was not an option?
3) What immediate actions can you take to overcome and push past procrastination?
4) What does the finished outcome and product look like?

CHAPTER FOUR

FEAR TRAPS

"Fear will always knock on your door. Just don't invite it in." Max Lucado

---

When I was 11 years old, I had to have surgery on my feet. I was unsure if I would ever be able to walk normal again. It started with me having severe pain in my feet for almost an entire year. I could barely wear shoes without being extremely uncomfortable. My grandmother suggested I get surgery, although everything in me was afraid to. I had never had surgery before, and this was the first time I would be on an operating table. Following the surgery, I would have to wear surgical braces for several weeks to heal. I thought, "What if the surgery goes bad? What if the kids at school tease and laugh at me? Will I ever walk again? Will I ever be able to dance again?" All of these fears and anxieties flooded my mind. I loved to dance and was always on my feet. I was also very athletic and played on the girls' basketball team around that time. All these thoughts overwhelmed me for weeks before the surgery. Anxiety and fear gripped me.

The morning of my operation, I was hysterical. The doctors had to give me some medicine in the lobby, to calm me down before I even went in the room. Looking back at this, I can now laugh. I was a little over the top. Yet at that moment, it was one of the scariest times of my life.

I went through with the surgery, and it was successful. After several long and difficult weeks of recovery, my feet eventually healed. As I reflect back, I am so grateful I went through with the operation. Today I can run, flip, dance, and do almost anything on my feet without pain! Several years after the operation, I moved to Los Angeles. God began to open doors for me to be featured in many athletic commercials and global print campaigns, including Nike, Diadora, and with several other fitness brands that required me to use my feet and run. Looking back, all of those nights I spent worrying and in fear, were pointless. God knew what the future would hold for me, and having that surgery prepared me for it.

What is fear? In modern society, fear is widely defined as an unpleasant emotion, caused by the belief that someone or something is dangerous, and likely to cause pain or a threat. The acronym of fear is also often recognized as false evidence appearing real. When conducting some research on the topic of fear and how to overcome it, some professionals recommended medication, some suggested life coaching, and some doctors even suggested being hypnotized.

Fear paralyzes 99% of people in the world. As a result, it keeps people from emerging into who they really want to be. Why is it that fear paralyzes so many? Why is it that it has the power to hinder people from pursuing their dreams? Why does fear seem to have so much influence and control over people's lives?

Did you know when you don't conquer fear, fear will conquer you?

> *You only have two options in life. You can either allow fear to be your master, or you can become the master of your fears.*

"God's Spirit doesn't make cowards out of us. The Spirit gives us power, love, and self-control." 2 Timothy 1:7 (CEV)

When God created us, He didn't give us the spirit of fear but of power, love, and a sound mind. What does this tell us? Fear is a spirit, and every day it's looking to intimidate, torment, paralyze you, and keep you stuck. Fear's number one goal is to keep you from emerging. It's the greatest threat to your destiny. However, once you open your mouth and speak back to fear, you become its master. You have authority over fear, and that power lies between your lips and what you speak and declare on a day-to-day basis. If you don't put fear in its place, it will keep you in a place of stagnancy, self-pity, worry, anxiety, doubt, depression, and shame.

Exploiting Fears Hiding Place

The first step to overcoming fear is identifying its source and root. The root of all fear is *unbelief.* Fear is the result of a lack of faith. It's the direct opposite of faith. Faith believes. Fear doubts. The reason why many people do the things they do in life is simply because they don't have faith. They don't believe. They meditate on the worst-case scenario, instead of the best-case scenario. They put their trust more in the illusion of fear, than they do faith. Because after all, fear is just an illusion, a deceptive appearance or impression. When you don't believe that you will ever be successful, and happy in your life or career, that's what you will get. We become what we meditate on.

"And now, dear brothers and sisters, one final thing. Fix your thoughts on what is true, and honorable, and right, and pure, and lovely, and admirable. Think about things that are excellent and worthy of praise." Philippians 4:18 (NLT)

We are to fix our thoughts on what's good. When you set your mind to meditate on what's inspirational, pure, honorable, right, true, lovely, excellent, and worthy of praise, your entire outlook on life will begin to change. Fear will become irrelevant.

Consider the relationship between a father and a child. A child has no reason to fear or doubt a loving parent that cares for them and nurtures them. They simply trust them, because they know their father has their best interest at heart.

I was raised by my dad growing up in Chicago. My dad always made sure he provided for his children. Thankfully I never questioned whether there would be food on the table, or if I would have some where to rest my head. I never questioned or doubted whether he could provide. Not because we were extremely rich, but because I knew he was committed to fulfilling his responsibility and becoming the best father he could. I trusted his word and promises to me. Fear was never present because there was never any unbelief. In the presence of my father's love, I had no reason to fear.

In the same way I trusted my father, how much more can we trust God, our Heavenly Father, to take care of us. God loves us, and because of His great love for us, we have no reason to fear. When you truly trust, fear cannot be present. That's why the Scriptures say that "perfect love drives out fear" 1 John 4:18 (NIV). Fear and love cannot dwell in the same atmosphere. When you choose love, when you choose faith, fear will no longer have a hiding place.

Only Believe

I have found that the only way to cancel out fear, is simply to only believe. This principle can be defined as suspending all doubt and unbelief in exchange for pure faith. It requires you to cancel out everything that is not done in faith. It demands you to forsake and abandon all roads that lead you to fear and doubt. Only believing is not just a mindset, it's a lifestyle.

An example of this is a moment when Jesus was traveling through a crowded town. A man named Jairus had a daughter who had become sick and just died. When Jesus arrived at his house, everyone was wailing and mourning. Jesus spoke to the crowd and said, "Don't be afraid. Only believe. She will be healed," Luke 8:50 (CSB). Jesus spoke and said, "She is not dead but asleep," Luke 8:52 (NIV).

Assuming Jesus was only joking, they laughed and ridiculed Him.

Jesus entered the room and behold a miracle was about to take place. Jesus grabbed the girl by the hand and spoke with authority, "My Child, get up!" Luke 8:53 (NIV). And at once, life was restored to the young girls cold and lifeless body. She got out of the bed and was reunited with her father. Jesus made a single declaration, and everything changed. Everyone was astonished and stared in awe. They were speechless. Yet, the people that stood in faith, and only believed, rejoiced with Him.

They had just become eyewitnesses to the miraculous power of God. As a result of faith, she was raised from death to life. In the same manner as Jesus, when you only believe, you have the power to speak to things that are dead, and declare that they come back to life. Faith has resurrection power.

"Death and life are in the power of the tongue, and those who love it will eat its fruits." Proverbs 18:21 (ESV)

You have in life, exactly what you speak and declare. If you speak death, nothing will flourish around you. When you speak life, however, everything will flourish around you. This Scripture ought to be the standard you live by in life. Despite how things may look around you, only believe. Speak life to every situation and circumstance. Only believe the best for your life. Only believe that your hard work will pay off. Your unwavering faith, combined with prayer and action, is the recipe to success. Faith and prayer, met with expectation, will always yield life changing results.

I remember one time I was counseling a friend through a difficult time. She was suicidal and wanted to end her life. That day, if I had not spoken to her, I am unsure if she would still be alive today. She was at rock bottom. As I began to ask questions, I identified the root of her problem. She began to confess how poorly she was treated by people during her childhood, and began quoting word from word, the mean things people had said about her all her life. She began to breakdown in uncontrollable tears, as she relived the horrible nightmares of her past.

Her childhood memories tormented her and made her fearful about the future. She was conflicted in her identity because she believed all the names, titles, labels, and ultimately lies, people spoke over her. She allowed every other voice to drown out the only voice that truly matters in life, God's voice. All she saw was the negative words, and as a result, this had kept her stagnant almost all her life. She became afraid to pursue and take action on anything. She became paralyzed by the fear of people.

A couple of years later, I had met a young woman. She shared her story with me of how she was recently diagnosed with a rare disease. Many thought that she wasn't going to make it and was going to die. This was challenging for her, but she was determined to live her best life, and never see the sickness as an obstacle. She was determined to see it as an opportunity to come out victorious and witness the healing power of God. She believed that life and death are in the power of your tongue and that what you meditate on, you become. As a result, she never allowed the negative words of other people to alter, define, or shape her reality. Every time someone had something negative to say, she rejected those words by replacing it with the Word of God and other positive affirmations.

Less than twelve months later, God healed her, leaving all her doctors in absolute shock. She walked away joyful, happy, and thankful. Today, she is extremely successful and living out her dreams.

Imagine if you rejected every negative word people tried to speak over your life, and only replaced them with the Word of God and positive declarations?

Instead of focusing on what can go wrong, it's time to start focusing on what can go right. The answer to gaining victory over fear is just that simple. Believe! Believe! Believe!

It's time to reset your mind and renew your perspective. When you can reset your mind, you can reset your life. It's time to get your joy and energy back, your passion back, and your zeal for life back. Don't let anyone else continue to deposit bad seeds into the garden of your life. No longer allow any source of fear, to take root. Start hanging around people that truly celebrate you, and people that push you to succeed. Start hanging around more like-minded people that have similar goals and desires. Start positioning yourself around people that are creative, driven, and inspirational. Change the diet of the information that you digest daily. Be more intentional about what you listen to and what you watch. Nourish yourself daily with only what feeds your soul. Not what starves it.

Fear Decoded: Fear Triggers

1.) Fear of Failure

The fear of failure paralyzes and holds people back from trying new things, taking risks, and pursuing their goals. They may have experienced failure in the past and have become afraid to try again. They fail to see their mistakes as simple learning lessons for future growth and development. This ultimately stunts their personal growth and keeps them from emerging.

2.) Fear of Rejection

The fear of rejection is birthed from the idea or feeling of not being wanted or accepted. This fear involves dread and avoidance as a result of past trauma. Rejection can have emotionally detrimental results on a person's self-esteem, and have a severe and unhealthy impact on their relationships with others.

3.) Fear of Success

The fear of success is the number one fear that keeps people from emerging. It causes people to sabotage their own success. They are afraid of public attention, and the spotlight that success brings. People in this category are afraid to take risks and move beyond their comfort zone. They also avoid new opportunities. As a result, people who have this fear often procrastinate and neglect personal and professional growth, and improvement. This person is afraid of how far their true potential and ability can actually take them.

4.) Fear of Judgment

The fear of judgment is driven by the fear of being ridiculed. People in this category are afraid of what people will say and how they will respond to their personal growth and success. As a result, many people play it safe and never aim very high in life. They are caught in the trap of people pleasing.

5.) Fear of Pain & Loss

The fear of pain and loss is gripping. Whether it's the fear of losing a loved one, losing a job, or losing a seemingly great opportunity, this fear paralyzes people, stirs high anxiety, and/or often causes emotional numbness.

6.) Fear of Abandonment and Isolation

The fear of abandonment and isolation stems from childhood loss, trauma, and/or abuse. People who suffer from this often distance themselves from getting too close to people and have a hard time building close relationships. On the contrary, they can also be needy, overly dependent on others, and lack a clear understanding of healthy boundaries. The fear of abandonment and isolation negatively impact relationships, whether intimate, social, or professional.

7.) Fear of Self-Expression

The fear of expressing your true self is driven by the fear of people. You become a slave to their opinions, mask who you truly are, and how you really feel. Additionally, many people don't reveal who they truly are, because deep down they don't feel like they are "enough." The fear of expressing your true self, can result in people spending their entire life seeking to live in the shadows of someone or something else, therefore never allowing their true self to shine.

8.) Fear of Intimacy

The fear of intimacy prevents people from getting close to others, and having healthy friendships, relationships, and marriages. People who experience this fear don't necessarily always want to avoid intimacy. Many desire it, but often push others away and sabotage good relationships. They frequently put up emotional walls, whether knowingly or unknowingly, and block people out.

9.) Fear of the Unknown

Many people resist change in response to the fear of the unknown. They fear anything that is outside their comfort zone. This fear creates mental blocks which influence the way we live our lives, and the decisions we make. This fear will hinder you from moving forward in life and has the potential to hinder your commitment to future goals, task, and obligations.

10.) Fear of Death

The fear of death is caused by abnormal and unhealthy thoughts of death and loss. It has a profound impact on our thoughts, feelings, and behaviors. This fear often keeps people from living life to their fullest potential. Death is inevitable, but your constant worry concerning it is something you have power over.

Take a moment and consider what fears have affected your life the most. Which fear triggers the most emotion? Write them down and explain why you feel this way. Write down the times, dates, places, people, and things associated with all your fears. Then, find a counselor or someone you trust, and talk about it with them. Analyzing your fears is the first step toward conquering them.

How To Overcome Fear

1.) Take Inventory of Your Fears

Write down your most common fears and why they have held you back. Journal about them openly and freely.

2.) Talk To Someone You Can Confide In

Find someone you can trust, or visit a counselor to help walk you through your journey. Having someone to talk about these issues with is crucial to emerging.

3.) Pray

You have authority over fear. You just have to open your mouth and declare your victory. Pray God's Word concerning your future. Meditate on Scriptures that fuel your confidence and faith. Only believe the good plans God has for your life. His plans are to prosper you and not harm you. Jeremiah 29:11 (NIV)

4.) Avoid Self-Sabotage

Don't allow fear to make you sabotage good opportunities. Always see things from a positive perspective. Look at the whole picture from an unbiased point of view, then make an educated decision.

5.) Respond

When you identify a fear trap, expose it, and verbally declare your victory over it – every single time. You must respond to fear and give it no room to speak.

6.) Only Believe

Wake up in the morning with an attitude that you are only going to believe the very best, regardless of past experiences or how you may feel. Suspend all doubt, and never lose hope.

7.) Be Brave

Be brave and bold in your pursuit of the future. Practice good courage every moment you can. Courage is like a muscle. It must be exercised daily.

8.) Develop New Morning Habits

How you start your day means everything. Every day you wake up, do it with zeal, energy, and passion. You may not always feel like it, but try and practice it. Cook breakfast in the morning with excitement, workout out with passion, and plan your day with enthusiasm. No more sluggishly inching through the morning!

9.) Be Present

Focus on breathing, listening, seeing, hearing, and being present in each moment you are gifted with. Take deep breathes often. Be grateful and don't complain. Learn how to find joy in your today. Matthew 6:34 (NIV) says, "Therefore do not worry about tomorrow, for tomorrow will worry about itself."

10.) Practice Gratitude

Be grateful for what you have and don't compare it to others. Someone, somewhere wishes they had the very things you complain about. Be thankful and always express gratitude.

Reflections

You have made it across the finish line. You are now equipped with everything you need to overcome fear. Take a moment and answer the questions below.

1) What areas are you struggling to believe in yourself?
2) What areas of your life do you feel "stuck" as a result of fear?
3) Who do you feel safe around that you can open up to about your fears?
4) What immediate actions can you take to overcome and push past your fears?

CHAPTER FIVE
EVOLVING SEASONS

"We cannot become what we want by remaining who we are."
Max Depree

Growing up in Chicago, I had the opportunity to witness all four seasons. Chicago is known for having very long winters, and extremely short summers. Being able to witness summer, fall, winter, and spring was always fascinating to me. I would carefully examine the leaves on the trees and watch them go from green in the summer, to orange in the fall, then disappear in the winter, and reappear in the spring. Every year, although the leaves would change, the trees would remain the same. The trees knew how to withstand change and knew how to navigate through the various seasons. These trees knew how to survive under the harsh pressures of their environment because that's what they were created to do. They were created to evolve with time.

To evolve means to change or develop gradually from a simple to a complex form. Evolving necessitates time, growth, and maturity. It requires you to consistently and confidently live on the wheel of change.

In the same way trees evolve and go through different seasons, we as people need to learn how to navigate through the different seasons of life with the same grace. We should expect change and embrace it, understanding that each new season, is beautifying us to a greater measure for the future.

There once was a man named David. He evolved from a young boy tending to his father's sheep in the fields, to a mighty warrior and king. Destiny didn't begin for David however when he took his seat on the throne to be king of Israel. It started in the green pastures while watching after his father's flock. David is known for the heroic story of defeating and killing Goliath. However, his early days were filled with many difficulties and challenges.

David is a man that can relate to the "invisible state" described in chapter one of this book. His older brothers were admired and respected, while David was left behind to do what seemed to be "the dirty work." It was in the sheep fields that God taught David everything he needed to know for his next level. It was in the fields he learned how to be still, hear God's voice, and obey. It was in isolation that he was being trained for greatness.

David was the youngest of eight sons. It may not have seemed like David would have a very bright future in the beginning, but as he began to evolve and step into his destiny, the tables turned.

It all began when Prophet Samuel, the son of our friend Hannah in chapter one, came to anoint the one God told him would be king. God gave Samuel specific instructions.

"But the LORD said to Samuel, "Do not consider his appearance or his height, for I have rejected him. The LORD does not look at the things people look at. People look at the outward appearance, but the LORD looks at the heart."

1 Samuel 16:7 (NIV)

On the outside, David appeared unqualified. Yet everything he had been through, prequalified him for the next level of his destiny. Once Samuel arrived at David's father's house, all the sons lined up. The Lord commanded and said to him, "You are to anoint for me the one I indicate." 1 Samuel 16:3 (NIV). David's father Jesse presented all seven of his sons to Samuel, except David. Then Samuel inquired about who was missing. When David finally arrived, the Bible says, "He was glowing with health and had an elegant appearance and handsome features." 1 Samuel 16:12 (NIV)

Then the LORD spoke to Samuel and said, "Rise and anoint him; this is the one." 1 Samuel 16:12 (NIV)

"So Samuel took the horn of oil and anointed him in the presence of his brothers, and from that day on the Spirit of the LORD came powerfully upon David." 1 Samuel 16:13 (NIV)

That was the day everything had changed for David. God had

chosen what appeared to be the least of the sons, to emerge as one of the greatest kings and leaders of his time. David went from being last, to becoming first. However, the promise wasn't delivered overnight. Studies say David was between 8 and 15 when he was first anointed to be King. There was still much development he had to undergo before he could sit and take his rightful place. There was an evolution that had to happen before he was to emerge into his greatness.

David had to wait at least 15 years from the time he was first anointed by Samuel, to the time he became king over Judah. David was thirty years old when he became king, and he reigned for forty years.

We live in a world today, where everyone desires to be famous overnight. Everyone is looking for a fast track way to success. Yet, there is an order that things need to happen in if you want lasting success. It takes time for you to emerge into the person you are called to be. It necessitates patience. Many people get discouraged and give up because it seems as if what they desire, is taking too long to happen. However, when you allow time, and your experiences to process you, and let patience have its perfect work in you, you will then be in the perfect position to emerge. Like David, you have been chosen and anointed by God. And at the right time, God will position and elevate you greater than you could ever position and elevate yourself. Trust God's timing and stay committed to the process.

In 2012, I had just graduated from George Washington University. I had studied journalism and mass communication and minored in theater and dance. I had completed several internships upon graduating and had built a lot of relationships in my field. Like most graduates, I had the "perfect" plan of how my future would look right after college, only to find myself three months later living back at home in my father's house in Chicago. I knew it was temporary, but the reality was challenging. It felt like all the plans I had were falling apart.

I had applied for thousands of jobs as a news reporter and did not hear anything back for months. I eventually got a temporary fill-in job working as a news reporter on the radio. I also picked up another job at a restaurant and worked that job until I figured out what my next step would be.

A couple of months later, I told my Father to pick up some moving boxes on his way home from work. He asked me why. I told him that I was getting ready to move to a new city and transition into the next phase of my postgraduate life. I honestly had no idea where I was going, but I knew that God would direct me. I received the moving boxes, packed up a few clothes, and set them by my bed. In faith, I prayed and asked God to show me the next step.

In February of 2013, I moved to Los Angeles with one suitcase and roughly $200 to my name. I had no job, and I had no idea how I was going to support myself.

I came because God showed me that He had a plan and assignment for me in that city. Thankfully, I had my brother, who had already been living in Los Angeles. He was gracious enough to let me come and stay with him. For the first seven months of my journey in Los Angeles, I slept on a floor mat in the corner of a one-bedroom apartment. I had no privacy and had to make do with the little space I had.

Within the first week I landed, I got plugged into a local church and started serving faithfully there. Shortly after I got an agent, expanded my skill set, took classes, and started acting. Starting out, I worked background on the sets of many movies and TV shows. Then, as I grew in knowledge and experience, I began booking roles, starring in national commercials, and hosting a variety of different talk shows and Hollywood red carpets. I began to emerge, and in L.A., I planted my roots.

I wasn't yet sure what the whole picture would look like. However, I was committed to evolving along the journey, and being open to whatever direction God would take me in.

In addition to acting, modeling, and hosting, I had always been a writer. I knew a part of my calling was to travel, speak, and write books. God began to show me visions of lives being changed and transformed through the books I would write, and places He would take me. It was incredible. I just trusted the process and knew one day it would all come together and make sense.

The Potter and the Clay

"Just like clay in the potter's hand, so are you in My hand." Jeremiah 18:6 (NIV)

Did you know that you are the clay and God is the potter? You are the clay in His hands. Every day, you are rotating on His potter's wheel, and He is shaping and molding you into exactly who you are supposed to be. Thinking about this excites me every time. You are reading this book because God is not done with you yet! Every day is a new day to be different from yesterday. No error you have done will keep God from working on you. When you allow God to fully take control, He will mold you and perfect you for His glory.

"For we are God's masterpiece. He has created us anew in Christ Jesus, so we can do the good things He planned for us long ago." Ephesians 2:10 (NLT)

You are God's masterpiece. Another translation says you are His workmanship. He will forever be at work in you. Don't let people put a period in your life, where God has only put a comma. It's okay not to have all the answers and not have it all figured out. Release control and take delight in not knowing. You are not God, and you aren't supposed to know.

To emerge, we must learn how to evolve. Let's look at some practical steps on how to embrace change.

Steps To Evolving

1.) Accept The Reality of Where You Are

Take a moment and take an honest assessment of where you are in life. Don't try and pretend to be in a place that you are not. Look at and examine what's real and accept it.

2.) Create Change & Make New Routines

Don't wait for change, create it. Evolving requires letting the past go. Explore new things. Take a new risk. Create new opportunities. Allow change to excite, inspire, and motivate you.

3.) Create

Evolving requires you to consistently create and produce new results. Focus on producing new ideas, content, and strategies. The deeper you dive into the production process, the less time you have to worry about outside distractions and other people's opinions.

4.) Shed Your Old Layers

Who you are becoming may be drastically different from who you used to be. You must be willing to shed old layers and be open to the newness each new season brings.

5.) Never Stop Evolving

Never let people, things, or circumstances, stunt your growth and keep you from emerging. Never stop learning and never stop challenging yourself to go higher. Continue to love and embrace various phases of change.

Reflections

The most beautiful part of life is evolving into the person you know you are called to be. Take a moment and answer the questions below.

1) What growing pains have I experienced in the process of evolving?

2) Where have I put a period in my life, where God has only put a comma?

3) What does success look like for me?

4) What does the new "me" in this season look like?

CHAPTER SIX
LOVE & WHOLENESS

"The purpose of our journey is to restore ourselves to wholeness."
Debbie Ford

On the morning of June 14th, 2011, I was awakened by a dream. All my friends went home during the summer months, while I stayed and worked a summer job at the university. At this time, I was in a long-distance relationship with a guy that I had been dating for two years. It was the first time in my life that I thought I was actually "in love." We both met in our hometown, our families knew each other, and at the time I felt that it was the perfect set up for us to one day marry, ride off on our white horse into the sunset, and live happily ever after. When reality hit, however, let's just say it hit hard.

He was cheating on me.

For an entire year, he had secretly been seeing someone else that I had no idea about. That day, I had never found myself so distraught in my life.

I was in my dorm room and had a roommate at the time that just moved in, and whom I barely knew. She was the only one there that night when I found out the news. I remember dashing into the living room in tears shouting, "Wake me up, I am dreaming!" As reality began to unfold, I lost it, and began to emotionally unravel. I continued, "Hit me! This can't be real!" I grabbed my roommate's hand and attempted to force her to slap me in the face. She paused and looked at me as if I had lost my mind. For a second, I did. Thankfully, she refused to slap me back to reality and calmed me down. As my tears quickly escalated into weeping, the revelation of this truth eventually brought me to my knees. I had a dream that morning that I found out he was cheating on me, and less than a few hours later, it all came to the light. I felt as if a hundred daggers had pierced straight through my heart. I felt broken and hopeless.

That week I couldn't eat. I had completely lost my appetite for food. I can still remember the chocolate banana walnut cake that I had baked, sitting in my refrigerator and rotting.

With the loss of that relationship, came the loss of the identity I had created. I created this false identity that I had it all "together" while really, I was broken, lost, and longing to be whole. I felt as if my life no longer had any meaning. It's funny how a breakup can do that to you huh?

I had been using this relationship as a shield to hide behind all my own fears and insecurities.

I had been using this relationship as a crutch, to keep me from seeking who I truly was, without all the "filters." I could no longer hide. It was the first time in my life that I had felt a way my pride had never allowed me to feel – weak and vulnerable.

To know true love, you must know heartbreak.

Heartbreak Facts

1. The brain does not differentiate between physical pain and extreme emotional pain.
2. The intensity and longevity of a heartbreak tend to be much more significant in women.
3. The physiological effects of heartbreak are similar to the physiological effects of a drug addict withdrawing from cocaine. Love is a drug.
4. You can either gain or lose a lot of weight while experiencing a heartbreak.
5. You will get over it and have the ability to move on.

Looking back, I am grateful for that heartbreak. It forced me to truly look in the mirror. I went from being a young and insecure girl to a woman knowing her worth and what she deserves. I had to be crushed first, however, to emerge into this place.

Emerging requires crushing.

If you have lived long enough, your heart may have been broken. If it hasn't, brace yourself. It is a part of the circle of life. For those who have, you may have been let down by someone you loved and put your trust in. Yet the good news is, God is a God of restoration and redemption. He heals broken hearts and will allow us to go through certain experiences to build us and shape us.

One critical pillar to becoming whole, is healing from past romantic relationships and/or walking away from unhealthy ones. Nothing has hindered a person from emerging more, than being entangled in relationships that take them off course. Who you choose to partner with, will steer the entire direction of your life.

Heart Exam

One afternoon I was outside doing yard work, and I caught a splinter. I looked at my finger, and it appeared to be a tiny piece of wood nestled in between my skin. If you ever had a splinter, you know how annoying it can be.

Getting a splinter may seem like no big problem. Yet, depending on how bad it is, it can be very aggravating and uncomfortable!

After at least thirty minutes of attempting to get it out, I finally came across some tweezers and extracted it from underneath my skin. I was finally relieved. Once removed, it felt as if it was never even there, and I carried on about my day. In this same way, when it comes to love, many of us have splinters in our heart. Some are deeper than others. Each splinter represents someone or something that hurt us in love. To emerge into love and achieve wholeness, healing must fully take place. You must give yourself time and space to heal. Whether it be family, friends, or former romantic partners, for these splinters to be removed, we must forgive, heal, and truly let go.

God created us for relationship. He designed us to be in healthy and thriving relationships. A healthy relationship requires communication, understanding, patience, forgiveness, and trust. It requires two people who are fully committed to the process and journey of love.

Love has been one of the most significant forces behind the most powerful unions we have seen in history up until this day. From the union of former President Barack and Michelle Obama to Jay Z and Beyoncé, it is evident that when you align with the right mate, you have the potential to soar and flourish like never before.

The evidence is also true on the reverse. Being aligned with the wrong partner can hinder you from the true destiny God has for you. Therefore, healing from past heartbreaks and relationships is essential.

What you don't heal from, will keep you from emerging into the next level of your destiny.

When you don't heal, you put yourself in a position to sabotage future relationships. Take a moment and consider if you have any splinters from past relationships and hurts that need to be removed. Consider the areas where you have talked yourself into believing you are "over" what happened to you, when deep down, you are not. Think about the areas that are still sensitive and difficult to talk about with others. Where are your sore spots?

We have a tendency as people, to leave the doors of past relationships cracked open, in the event, fear bullies us to retreat back. Fear that we may never find anyone else. Fear that we will end up lonely for the rest of our lives. Fear that the next person may not be able to accept the "you" with all the scars, hurt, pain, and damage.

Forgiving people that hurt you both intentionally and unintentionally can be challenging to accomplish. Yet once done, it will break unhealthy emotional cycles, barriers, and patterns that are holding you back from experiencing true love.

Stephanie Rische, the senior editor of nonfiction books at Tyndale House Publishers, once wrote, "When we endure these heartbreaks ourselves—rejection, betrayal, abandonment—we don't walk through them alone. God has walked that road Himself. And in some mysterious way, when our hearts are broken, we're given new insight into the very character of God."

One day a woman told me the story of how she married a man. At first, it appeared to be a perfect life. Her husband was well respected in his industry, and she was highly esteemed and sought after as his wife. However, over time, that beautiful portrait of love began to fade. They began to constantly disagree and fight, and love was no longer the center of their union.

Soon after, the couple divorced. She found herself questioning whether she was even worthy of being loved again.

With time, she began to heal after the divorce. She stopped blaming herself for everything that went wrong. She began to go through the process of rediscovering her own voice and strength. In due time, she began to emerge as the confident woman she had always been. She began to open her heart to love again, and one day without even trying or seeking out love, a new love found her. She met someone new that made her forget about her past. Now, they are happily married. I believe God opens doors and will give us all another chance at finding true love.

Love requires you not being afraid to try again.

Benefits of Love

1.) You Live Longer

According to the National Health Interview Survey, single and unmarried people face a 58% higher risk of mortality in any given year.

2.) Healthier Heart Condition

The physical condition of your heart is better when you are in a happy union and lessens the likelihood of heart attacks.

3.) You Age Better

Those who are in happy unions are proven to look, feel, and age better compared to those who are not.

4.) Less Stress

You are often calmer, have less anxiety, and/or deal with stress a lot better.

5.) Happier Life

Every relationship has its ups and downs. Yet it's proven that people in unions live a happier life overall.

Becoming Whole is Our Responsibility

Pursuing wholeness should be our number one goal on the journey to emerging. Wholeness requires taking time to nourish your body, mind, soul, and spirit daily. Wholeness is about feeding every part of you on a consistent basis. It's about leaving no aspect of your emotional, spiritual, and mental well-being untouched. It's about focusing on and giving careful attention to every part of you daily.

Many people in life allow themselves to play the "victim" role as a result of their pain. They resist growth and change because of past pain they experienced. Adopting this way of thinking is not only unhealthy, but will affect every relationship around you. People who aren't actively seeking out how to be healthy, whole, and restored, often end up tearing down the people around them, as a result of their pain and brokenness. Your wholeness contributes to the prosperity of everyone connected to you. When you begin to actively seek out how to become whole, the entire world takes notice. You become an active contributor to society and add value everywhere you go.

Becoming whole is about aiming to achieve wholeness in every area of your life and existence. Does this mean you are perfect? No. However to emerge, we want to strive to be whole in our physical bodies and health, in our spiritual lives, in our way of thinking, in our relationships (personal, professional, and romantic) and in our careers. Wholeness is a lifelong journey.

You may be reading this and have just gotten out of a relationship and trying to pick up the pieces of your life again. You may be single and looking for love. You may even already be happily married. Whatever stage you are at, aim to be healed, whole, and content.

Your brokenness is the most precious and valuable thing you can give to God. God desires to heal us and make us complete in Him.

Steps to Wholeness

1.) Forgive

Make a list of everyone that has hurt you. Call them, text them, and reach out to them. Let them know you forgive them and mean it. If you find it difficult to forgive, pray, and ask God to help you and show you. He will give you the courage and strength.

2.) Don't Be Easily Offended

We live in a world where people often get easily offended. This offense can often escalate into disagreements, arguments, and ultimately violence. Don't be easily angered by the offense. Don't let people shift you off track. Allow offense and negative words to easily roll off your back.

3.) Discipline Your Emotions

Never allow your emotions to run your life. To be whole, you must learn how to discipline and train your emotions. Proverbs 16:32 (BSB) says, "He who is slow to anger is better than a warrior, and he who controls his temper is greater than one who captures a city." You must learn healthy emotional balance.

4.) Cast Your Cares Upon God

Cast every fear and worry you have unto God. Many people try to hold on to their pain and emotional baggage. These people get burned out and are easily overwhelmed in life. Make it an effort through prayer, to release your cares onto God every single day.

5) Shift Your Focus

You become what you meditate on. If you meditate on social media every day and always compare yourself, you will forever be in a state of unhappiness.

Your mind is a sponge. It's continuously absorbing information. Philippians 4:8 (NLT) says, "Fix your thoughts on what is true, and honorable, and right, and pure, and lovely, and admirable. Think about things that are excellent and worthy of praise."

6.) Be Led By Peace

On your journey to wholeness, you have to guard your heart and mind. Cast down every thought that makes you retreat back to who you used to be. Philippians 4:7 (NIV) says, "And the peace of God, which transcends all understanding, will guard your hearts and your minds in Christ Jesus." Let the peace of God lead you.

Reflections

Take a moment and examine the areas you desire true healing and wholeness. Consider every splinter your heart has experienced. Answer the following questions. Do an honest assessment and don't hold back.

1) Would you describe yourself as healed and whole?
2) Is there anyone in your life that you have not released the full measure of forgiveness to?
3) Who have you hurt in the past that may desire an honest apology from you?
4) How have experiences from your past potentially affected your relationships with other people?
5) How can you experience more happiness and fulfillment right now in your current relationships?

CHAPTER SEVEN

THE BLUEPRINT TO SUCCESS

*"The plans of the diligent lead surely to abundance, but
everyone who is hasty comes only to poverty."*
Proverbs 21:5 (NIV)

What makes a person truly diligent? Diligence can generally be
defined as a constant and earnest effort to accomplish a
desired goal with persistent exertion of body, mind, and skill.
Diligence is working smarter and not harder. It is doing your
work efficiently with excellence in a timely manner. Diligence
is paying attention to the details and finding creative ways to
solve problems. Diligence requires your full commitment day
in and day out.

Proverbs 12:24 (NIV) tells us, "The hand of the diligent will
rule." To rule means to control, dominate, lead, and govern.
When you actively apply the principle of diligence to your life,
you will never lack. Diligence gives you the upper hand and
will position you in a place of power, influence, and authority.
When you are diligent, you will not lack anything, and
experience ever-increasing success.

To emerge, you must master diligence.

It takes diligence to produce and get the results you are seeking out of life. Diligence is not about starting and stopping, it's about starting and finishing.

Diligence requires you to go the extra mile - every single day. Many people, however, don't want to go the extra mile in life. People will often complain and say, "It's just too hard." Your breakthrough, however, is in that "extra" mile. If you do not persevere, the fullness of your dreams will never be realized.

Your win is in the extra mile.

Often times, when a person goes to the gym, going that extra mile on the treadmill seems impossible. You feel like you are at your breaking point. Yet when you fight and push until the end, the reward is so much sweeter. Diligence will unlock the doors that have been locked in your life for all too long. Go the extra mile.

The Secret To Becoming More Diligent

1.) Self-Discipline

Self-discipline is the ability to exercise restraint, self-correct, resist temptation, endure during difficult times, be consistent, abandon immediate pleasure for long-term benefits, and successfully govern your life. Proverbs 25:28 (NIV) says, "A man without self-control is like a city broken into and left without walls." To be "without walls" is to be without protection or defense, ultimately leaving you vulnerable to outside attacks, that will hinder your progress as you strive toward success.

2.) Build Character

Character is who you are when people aren't watching. Your attitude, beliefs, morals, temperament, and overall personality traits all make up a persons' character.

4.) Develop The Leader Within

Every day, you must sharpen and develop your leadership skills. You must surround yourself with other leaders that will help sharpen and challenge you in every area of your life.

5.) Removing Distractions

Diligent people aggressively eliminate distractions. They don't make excuses and do not allow distractions to hinder their progress. Too much time on social media, your phone, and watching TV, are common distractions that hold people back from achieving their goals. Whether it be people, places, or things, avoid distractions like the plague. Give them no room in your life.

6.) Skillful Management

When you can skillfully manage every resource in your life, diligence will promote you. Become an expert at managing your time, your money, and resources. Take record of everything. Be meticulous and let nothing go overlooked. Organize and prioritize your life. Work on continually improving your management skills and you will skyrocket in success.

Your Difference is Your Weapon

No person will ever be the "you" God created. Your difference is designed to set you apart from the crowd and promote you. Don't forsake the 'you' God created by trying to be a clone of somebody else. In this next season, it's going to be your difference that elevates you. You must own and walk in what distinctly sets you apart. Diligence, along with walking in the power of your difference, will position you to emerge in influence and power.

What's Your Why?

What's your why in life? What drives you? Is it family? Your faith? Your children? Your career? Your "why" is the fuel to keep your vision alive. Once you lose sight of what's driving you, you lose fuel. Yet when you meditate on your "why" daily, it will keep you focused and hold you accountable to your vision.

Most people give up and burn out in life because they forget why they started. Eventually, their passion begins to diminish because they did not hold fast to the vision and keep their "why" in focus.

Just like a plant, you have to nurture your "why" daily. There have been many instances in my life where I wanted to give up and quit. However, when I was able to reach into the depths of who I really was, walk in the power of what made me different, and remember my "why,'" a warrior began to arise within me. Know your "why" and don't forget it.

Wise Counsel

In today's world, everyone wants to make their own rules and create their own path. We cannot, however, neglect those who paved the way for us. Many of us fail to seek out wise counsel because we simply think we know it all. Wake up call. You don't. I don't care how many degrees you have, or how much your net worth is, the key to continued growth and development is mentorship. The Bible says, "For through wise counsel you will wage your war, and victory lies in an abundance of advisors." Proverbs 24:6 (NIV)

Seeking wise counsel will help you avoid the mistakes of those who went before you. It is the smartest, fastest, and most strategic way to progress in any area of your life.

From Oprah Winfrey to Michael Jordan, they all had mentors. To get to where you are going, you need to collaborate with someone who has already walked that path. Good mentors will help guide you in your decision-making process. It is true. If you hang around the wise, you will become wise. The opposite is also true. If you hang around fools, you will become a fool.

Mastering Your No

To emerge, you must learn how to confidently say no. Have you ever found yourself tired and overwhelmed because you have given out too many "yes's'" to people? I have learned that a person that doesn't know how to master saying no, does not know how to master his or her own life.

Mastering your no requires vision and discipline.

The word "no" means to reject and refuse approval. The word "no" represents a line in the sand between what stands within your boundaries, and what exists outside of them. Boundaries are vital. Like a seatbelt, they protect you. To deliver your no with confidence, you must first have developed a thorough understanding of your personal boundaries. Your personal boundaries must become laws in your life. Laws that you don't compromise and don't exempt people from. These are what I call your non-negotiables. It is crucial that you have them.

When you begin to give your yes to everyone, it begins to lose its value. Your yes becomes like playdough in someone's hands, and they can bend and stretch you in whatever way they like.

Many of us have allowed people to rob us of our no, to only walk out of a room with a yes that brings us much despair. If I had known the power of my no earlier, I would have used the word a lot more often.

"But let your 'Yes' be 'Yes' and your 'No', 'No.' For whatever is more than these is from the evil one." Matthew 5:37 (NKJV)

Many people in the world have a hard time saying no. Some people have a hard time saying no because they genuinely are nice and hate to disappoint people. However, you must raise your standards. Everyone and everything does not deserve your yes. Growing up, telling people no was tough for me. Naturally, you want to please everybody. You don't want to let anyone down because you want to prove to him or her, that you care, and that you're a good person. However, who said you couldn't master your no and still be a good person?

A "yes man" is defined as a person who agrees with everything said. Saying yes is easy, but taking a stand and saying no requires a different level of confidence. A person that can let their 'yes' be 'yes' and 'no' be 'no' as Matthew 5:37 says, is a person of true power and authority.

Benefits of Mastering Your No

1.) Mastering your no helps you save time. Time is valuable, and you can't get it back. Being upfront is the best way you can be.

2.) Mastering your no will help launch you into an entirely new level of emotional, spiritual, psychological, and physical freedom.

3.) Mastering your no will help you put an end to people pleasing.

4.) Mastering your no will help you avoid distractions.

5.) Mastering your no will help deliver you out of compromising situations.

6.) Mastering your no is a seed for your future.

Your Agenda For The Next Level

1.) Make God Your Business Partner

Make a decision that you are going to invite God into your daily decision-making process. From how to manage your time, to how to divide your resources, ask God daily for wisdom. He will help you navigate and avoid pitfalls. He will give you the vision and direction you need for the next step.

2.) Know Your Why

Take the time today to write down the vision for your life and/or revise your current vision or plan. Write down your goals, plans, and aspirations for every area of your life in detail. Consider your lifestyle, faith, health, family, marriage, career, and business. Combine all these things and organize them in a place you can see them.

3.) Plan of Action

Now create a plan of action. Write down three immediate courses of action you can take to move your vision forward. Continue to do this until the fulfillment of each goal.

4.) Seek Mentors

As I mentioned earlier, find a mentor. Throughout my life, I have had many mentors. I have had both career mentors and spiritual mentors. Both are necessary to succeed in life. You need wise counsel. Don't let pride and thinking you know everything, keep you from seeking out mentors. No matter how experienced you think you are, always connect and build relationships with people that have your answer, and not your problem.

5.) Ask and Receive

After you have put in the work, applied diligence, and put in the time, don't be afraid to ask for help if you need it. We have not in life, because we ask not.

It's In Your DNA to Win

Did you know that when God created you, He put every

resource within you to win on every level in life?

You are wired to succeed. God has already given you all the tools you need. Refuse to settle for less and refuse to make excuses. Be diligent and commit yourself to excellence. Your purpose is bigger than you. You can no longer afford to procrastinate. Don't put off tomorrow, what you can do today. To be great, you must act and respond now.

Reflections

Take a moment and examine the areas you desire to see greater measures of success in your life. Think about every area of your life that needs upgrades and improvement. Take a moment and answer the following questions.

1) Do you have a clear and concise plan for what you want to achieve?
2) What areas of your life do you need to exercise more diligence and discipline?
3) How can you change your morning routine to get better results out of your day?
4) How can you be a better manager of your time and resources?

CHAPTER EIGHT

THE PIT TO THE PALACE

"So the last will be first, and the first last."
Matthew 20:16 (NIV)

In 2017, I lost everything. My living arrangements in Los Angeles fell through at the last minute, and I had no time to prepare. As a result, I became homeless. I got a call, and within twenty-four hours, I had to make a decision. That decision was to either go back home to Chicago and quit, or stay in Los Angeles.

During the time I was homeless, I slept in my car. I had to work, go to all my auditions, and still try to look for a new place to live. I still had a full plate of responsibilities. However, I made no excuses and brought my A-game every single time. I showered at the Planet Fitness gym and set up a temporary mailbox to receive my mail. Most nights were very cold and often scary. Some nights I slept in parking lots. Some nights I parked and slept under a tree. Some nights I would sleep outside of mansions in Beverly Hills, not too far from Bel Air. Yet somehow through it all, I felt the peace of God surrounding me like never before. I was determined to emerge and never take my eyes off the prize.

Every day I would pray, speak over my life, and declare the

Word of God. "I am going from the pit to the palace!" I would say, not even realizing how powerfully my words were shaping my destiny. During that time, my faith was the only thing that gave me the courage and strength to persevere.

There were nights that I cried and wanted to lose hope. However, I would hear a small still voice whispering, "But those who wait on the Lord shall renew their strength; They shall mount up with wings like eagles; They shall run and not be weary; They shall walk and not faint." Isaiah 40:31 (NKJV)

I would hear the whisper of destiny saying, "Keep Going!"

One morning, I got a call from a woman that lived at the top of the hill in Bel Air. Bel Air is one of the most prestigious and wealthiest cities in the United States. Growing up I would watch the "Fresh Prince of Bel Air" on television starring Will Smith, but never knew much about the city outside of that. When I first moved to L.A., I would drive through the hills of Bel Air and just dream. I would walk around the neighborhood declaring and believing that one day, God would bring me into such a place of prosperity and wealth.

The woman that called me that morning had found out I was sleeping in my car through a mentor of mine. The woman and her family immediately took me in and showered me with so much love. They embraced me as if I was their own child.

Within 24 hours I went from sleeping in my car under a tree, just minutes from Bel Air, to sleeping in a mansion in the hills of Bel Air. I literally went from the "pit" to the "palace" overnight. I remember walking out into their backyard one day overlooking the entire city. What a beautiful sight it was. As I looked off into the distance, I began to weep. I was in awe of what God had done. Although it wasn't my house, I began to thank God for answering my prayers. He had not forgotten about me. All those nights sleeping in the car, only to be embraced by so much love, kindness, and compassion overwhelmed me. I thought if God could do that in 24 hours, what more can He do? What more will He do in my life?

During this season, it looked like I had lost everything. All the while, God was just getting started. A few weeks later, I got a call to do a pageant. It was a preliminary competition for the

Miss California USA pageant. Competing in a beauty pageant was the furthest thing from my mind at the time. I thought, "This is the last thing I need to be thinking about! I need to get back on my feet!" However, God had another plan in mind. Just days before the pageant, a stranger had sponsored my entire entry fee into this pageant and paid the cost in full. It was several hundred dollars. I was shocked. This was a total stranger who I eventually came to have the pleasure of meeting.

Less than five days later, I am competing in a pageant that I felt totally unready and unfit for. I was nervous and honestly felt uncomfortable, vulnerable, and insecure. I didn't feel qualified to compete after recently going through such a difficult time. I felt as if it was all happening too soon. Yet, I trusted that if God brought me to it, He would bring me through it.

I arrived at the pageant. Now, although my entry was paid for, there were many other personal items I needed that I didn't have. During the time I was homeless, I lost everything. Including most of my clothes and accessories. I arrived at the pageant with no gown to compete in. You heard me. No gown. Now if you have ever watched Miss USA, the evening gown competition is the most anticipated, by both the judges and the audience. To my surprise, the girls I was competing against started to come together and give me everything I was missing. Everything, except a gown.

I was backstage and was number three in line. The girls lined up in their beautiful and sparkling evening gowns. Meanwhile, I was sitting on my suitcase in a corner, thinking how in the world is this going to happen. I was just minutes away from having my name called on stage. Yet suddenly, just moments before I was set to walk on stage, something magical happened. A woman came running from the back and threw me a yellow gown. She said, "Put this on and get in line!" I put the gown on in a hurry without almost even giving myself a glance in the mirror. The dress was the perfect fit! I was back in the game. I got in line, took a deep breath, went on stage, and performed to the best of my ability. I thought to myself, win or lose, I am just glad I made it this far!

That night, the judges were giving out crowns and sashes for three different local cities, and one of those cities happened to be Bel Air. I didn't know if I was going to win and had no clue which city I would be crowned to represent. It's the final moments of the competition, and my heart is racing.

All of a sudden, I hear the show host announce, "And your new Miss Bel Air USA, is Chance Cessna!" My heart stopped. To say I was shocked is an understatement. How did I just go from sleeping in my car minutes from Bel Air, to becoming the queen of it?

I spent the next twelve months as an ambassador for the city, meeting some of the most influential people in the world and making unforgettable memories. God was blowing my mind with one experience after another. God showed me that every mountain, no matter how big it is in life, can be moved.

Miss Hollywood Pageant Winners Crowned
The Miss Hollywood, Miss Bel Air and Miss Central Coast Pageants took place on July 30 at the DoubleTree in Downtown Los Angeles. The next pageant will take place in October for the titles of Miss Calabasas USA and Los Angeles County USA. (L to R) Shaianne Powell (Miss Central Coast USA); Janella Garcia (Miss Hollywood Teen USA); KaitLynn Markley (Miss Bel Air Teen USA); Chance Cessna (Miss Bel Air USA); Ashley Thompson (Miss Hollywood USA); Aja Simms (Ms. Hollywood); Andrea McClew (Mrs. Hollywood); Jewell Negin (Ms. Bel Air)

Source: Beverly Hills Weekly Magazine

This moment represented something more profound than just winning a competition. It was bigger than audience applauses, fans, and cheers. It was God speaking loud and clear, that even when you feel weak and unqualified, I will prove myself strong. It's not about what you can do in your own strength, but what God has already paved the way to make possible.

"My grace is sufficient for you, for My power is made perfect in weakness." 2 Corinthians 12:9 (ESV)

My greatest setback led to my greatest breakthrough. On stage that day, I emerged. Not by my own might, but by God's grace.

Through all these experiences, God showed me His great love for me and how to trust Him through it all. He revealed to me the power of being vulnerable and weak. He taught me how to hold His hand and trust Him while I am still yet afraid. I did nothing to deserve this. It was simply just God's favor and mercy. I believe that when you decide to put your entire life in the hands of God, He will deliver you and set you up in a way no one or nothing else can.

Some of you reading this book right now may feel like you are in a pit. You may be in a place or a position where you are discouraged. Things around you may not look like you thought they should look by now. It may feel like no matter how much you try, things never seem to get better. However, let my story be a testament of how swiftly things can change in your favor. God can take you from the pit to the palace. You may feel like you are last now, but God has the power to make you first. You have the power to emerge. There is a palace with your name on it. Don't give up. You are almost there.

When you come into alignment with God's plan for your life, He can accelerate you faster than you can wrap your mind around. What took some people years to accomplish, you will be able to achieve within a fraction of the time because of His favor. There is nothing like divine acceleration to make up for all the years you missed as a result of lack of direction, faith, resources, or guidance.

There once lived a man named Joseph. He was the son of Jacob. Like King David, as a youth, he tended to his father's sheep in the fields. Joseph was the youngest of all his brothers and was special in his father's eyes because he had him at an old age. One day his father had a special gift made for him. It was a custom designed coat of many colors. It was beautiful, radiant, and crafted with excellence. Once his older brothers found out, they grew jealous and envious.

Then one night, Joseph had a dream. In this dream, God was showing him that he was going to promote him in his family, and he was going to reign in his land. He told his brothers, and they hated him even more. They became even more jealous, bitter, and envious, so much so they plotted to kill him. His brothers seized him and ripped off his coat of many colors and threw him into a deep empty pit to die.

Joseph ultimately ended up being sold into slavery in Egypt at just 17. Far away from his family, his future looked hopeless. As the story unfolds, while in Egypt, Joseph was falsely accused of raping his slaveowners wife. She lied and set up a trap for him. As a result, Joseph was put in jail.

Joseph endured much pain, sorrow, and disappointment throughout his journey, but he never gave up. Soon however, Joseph's day would finally come. His dream would finally be realized. All the years of pain and suffering would pay off. He was released from jail after interpreting an important dream for the King. Soon after, the tables began to turn in his favor. He went from being a slave in Egypt, to becoming the ruler of Egypt. At age 30, Joseph emerged into prominence and power like never before. Joseph emerged into his greatness as a result of his opposition.

Embracing The Unpredictable

Life is filled with unpredictable circumstances. Whenever we make plans in life, we must be open to them not turning out how we initially imagined them. Life simply will not always go the way that you have planned. And guess what? It's okay. When you allow yourself to be present and accept the surprises and curveballs that life throws at you, you will become more at peace with what the future holds for you. Life is much easier when you accept all the surprises it comes with.

It's important to plan and prepare, but be open to change. Practice being more present in the moment instead of trying to predict and control every single outcome. The detours of life may shift and direct you out of your comfort zone and into places you haven't been before. Go with it. The more you release control and trust God on your journey, the happier, more fulfilled, and at peace, you will become.

"And we know that all things work together for good for them that love God, to them who are called according to his purpose." Romans 8:28 (KJV)

When you are driving on the road in an unfamiliar area, the only thing you can do is trust the signs that guide you. In this same way, we must trust every sign and direction God gives us in life. He is our guide and map and will never lead you astray. He makes everything work together for our good.

Overcoming the Impossible

When I was eight years old, my mother was pronounced brain dead. She had suffered from a stroke while driving us home from a dentist appointment. While waiting for the ambulance, my mother lost too much oxygen to her brain. Soon after, she was placed on life support. It happened all too fast, and we had no control.

The doctors suggested they take my mother off life support. However, my grandmother was believing God for a miracle. My grandmother brought her home, hired nurses, and took care of her. To witness my mother in such a condition was one of the greatest challenges of my life.

What was supposed to be a couple of weeks on life support, turned into months, then turned into years. My mother was on life support for a shocking total of ten years.

For an entire decade, my grandmother kept the faith. However, when my mother's heart took its last beat in 2009, there was nothing else that could be done. We were no longer in control. God had finally called her home.

Releasing Control

How do you release control, in a world that tells you that you always need to be in control? As humans, we spend most of our lives making decisions and being in control. The idea of not being in control can be scary. So how do you walk that fine line of being in charge, yet simultaneously living a surrendered life? How can you trust even when you don't have all the answers?

We can learn to release control when we realize we were never really in control to begin with. Were you in control of the day you were born? Were you in control of the hospital you were born in, what time you were birthed, and how many hours your mother spent in labor? No. We were born with no control, and we will leave this earth with no control. No one knows when their time is up.

If we live and die without being in control, be assured that the God who created us, is in control and has a plan for our lives. Releasing control teaches you to trust, be at peace, and enjoy the ride.

Reflections

Think about every area of your life where you have been working overtime to control the outcome. Whether it be in your relationships, finances, your career, your family, or your marriage, meditate on these areas. Take a moment and answer the following questions. Be honest and don't be afraid to examine areas of your life where you are a control freak.

1) Do you trust God's plan for your future?
2) What areas of your life do you spend worrying the most?
3) When's the last time you fully released control while facing a challenge?
4) How can you start embracing the unpredictable?

CHAPTER NINE
EMERGE STORIES

"For with God, nothing shall be impossible."
Luke 1:37 (ESV)

When I started writing this book, I had a vision that it would not just be another book on the shelf, but that it would be a book that would ignite a fire and passion in the lives of people all across the world. I had a dream that this book would reach across borders, cultures, and religions and awaken dreams, passions, and desires that have quietly been lying dormant for far too long. I wanted to help people emerge and breakthrough into their God-ordained destiny.

Throughout this book, I have shared many of my own emerge stories. However, we all have a story. In the rest of this chapter, I will share some inspirational emerge stories that will give you inspiration and faith for your journey.

Emerge Story #1

This excerpt is from the book, "A Woman's Guide to Spiritual Warfare" by Quinn Sherrer & Ruthanne Garlock, in which a mother named Carrie, emerged from fear to victory, and witnessed the greatest miracle of her life.

"Matt grew increasingly angry and depressed because of conflict with his father, who often criticized him and rarely showed Matt any affection or approval. One day, as I was in prayer," [Carrie], said, "the Lord said to me, Great fear is coming upon you, but you will have the victory over it."

Carrie didn't know what that meant, but she increased in her prayer time, often praying Malachi 4:6, that God would turn her husband's heart toward his son Matt and vice versa.

That Fall, when Matt's senior year began, he was depressed because he did not like school, and he was upset that he did not have his own car. Carrie was troubled about his interest in a horror-film character, and by a poster he had placed in his room with an alien monster figure on it. Standing in his room, she would bind the evil spirits that were bringing oppression to her son.

Shortly after school started, a tenth grader in the community committed suicide by driving his car off a cliff. As Matt's depression got worse, he told his father that he felt his mind was about to snap. Carrie and her husband prayed in agreement, pleading the blood of Jesus over their son and asking God to protect him from suicide.

One morning, Carrie had a heart-to-heart talk with Matt about his depression and his girlfriend problems, then she shared some Scriptures with him before he left for school.

Throughout the day, she prayed Psalm 3:3 over him and asked God to raise up intercessors to pray for her son. Later that afternoon, when she returned from a shopping errand, she saw Matt as he was leaving for Bible study and choir practice.

"God bless you, son," she said. "Have a good time, and I'll talk to you tonight."

A few hours later, Matt drove his mother's car off a three-hundred foot cliff in the same area where the other boy had died, only higher up. He said goodbye to his girlfriend and then drove to the cliff to read the bible and pray in an attempt to reach God. Feeling there was no response, he started the car, rammed the accelerator and drove off the cliff.

As soon as the wheels left the road, Matt had realized that he had made a horrible mistake. Jesus, please forgive me, he prayed, thinking he was going to die. Take me home! He blacked out just before the car landed.

A woman living nearby saw what happened and phoned the police as the car crashed on the rocky seashore below.

Matt crawled from the wreckage in shock. Two Christian policemen walked up to him. "God must really love you, son," one of them said, "because He just saved your life."

These men had seen four or five other suicide attempts from that cliff. Matt is the only one who survived.

The policemen saw a Coast Guard helicopter overhead and signaled for help. "Who called you?" one officer yelled to the pilot over the noise as they lifted Matt into the chopper. "No one – I just happened to be in the area" the pilot answered.

Within minutes, Matt was in the trauma unit of a nearby hospital. When his parents arrived, he was unconscious and unable to talk. What Carrie had spoken over her son that afternoon came true. God did bless him by saving his life. Also, she did talk with him that night, and he was alive!

Matt came through the experience miraculously, only needing to wear a back brace for a few months. He received therapy from a Christian psychiatrist, who was mystified as to why Matt had taken such drastic action.

In the days following the crash, Carrie cried out to God one day, "Oh Lord, what was I doing at the exact moment of the crash?"

"That makes no difference, He replied. What made a difference was what you were doing before the crash."

In the years since the crash, Matt reconciled with his father and today, he is married with a family of his own.

Reflections

This story reflects the great compassion and never-ending love that God has for us even when we make mistakes. It reveals the power of a mother's faith and how she had to emerge using the weapon of prayer so her son could live. For years, Carrie would pray for her son and did not give up. If it weren't for her prayers, Matt might not have been alive today.

Emerge Story #2

Rob, a healthy college student and a young athlete, knew that his future was bright. Growing up with a passion for sports, he loved being active. One spring, while in school, he started having severe headaches. They began to come right after another. This led his mother to eventually take him to the hospital for the doctors to run some test. To the entire family's surprise, the doctor declared that Rob had cancer at just 20 years old. They found a small mass behind his nose. It was a rare form of cancer called nasopharynx. Using the focus, passion, determination, and resilience he learned from sports, he decided that he was not going to allow cancer to defeat him. He put his faith to action.

When he began radiation, he would walk into the hospital as if cancer was already defeated, because in his mind he had already won the battle.

Every day, he would speak positive affirmations over his health and life. He remained steadfast in prayer and hope. He did this almost every day for six months straight. After going through 28 radiation treatments in the summer of 2010, he got a call from the doctors saying that he was cancer free! He went to a follow-up doctor's appointment, and since that day, they have never found a trace of the disease. Today, Rob is healthy and active, and is the author of a book entitled "Win from Within: Discover the Champion Inside."

Reflections

Rob could have allowed fear to grip and paralyze him. Instead, he made a decision to emerge from fear to embrace hope. He challenged what appeared to be a threat to his destiny, and within only six months, he was completely healed from cancer! He declared positive affirmations and Scriptures daily. He believed God for His healing and received the answer to his prayer.

Emerge Story #3

Nick Vujicic was born in Melbourne, Australia. He was born with tetra-amelia, a rare disorder where a person is born without any arms or legs. He is one of the seven known surviving individuals in the world today who live with the syndrome.

According to his autobiography, his mother refused to see or hold him while the nurse held him in front of her, but she and her husband eventually accepted their son's condition and understood it as "God's plan for their son."

Initially, he was born with his toes on one foot fused together. An operation was performed to separate the toes so that he could use them as fingers to grab, turn a page, and perform other functions.

Nick once said at a conference he was speaking at "At age 10, I tried to commit suicide with 6 inches of water in my family bathtub. The first two times I rolled over, I was trying to work out how much air I could hold in my lungs before I let the water come in. On the third time I rolled over, I saw a picture in my mind of my mum, my dad and my brother crying at my grave, wishing they could have done something more. And that alone stopped me. I realized there is a pain of having a disabled son with no limbs, but greater is the pain to have a son without limbs who commits suicide."

After his mother showed him a newspaper article about a man dealing with a severe disability when he was seventeen, he started to give talks at his prayer group. This ignited a passion within him to emerge and share his story. He began to encourage others that there is nothing that can stop you from greatness.

Without any limbs Vujicic can write, type 45 words per minute, swim, answer the phone, and kick tennis balls exceptionally far.

In 2005 when he was 17, Vujicic founded Life Without Limbs, an international non-profit organization and ministry. This marked the beginning of him traveling across the world, reaching millions of people. He's traveled to more than 44 countries and inspires millions of people across the globe. Vujicic is now happily married with four healthy children.

Reflections

Nick Vujicic did not let the fact that he was born without legs and arms stop him from accomplishing his dreams. He used his disadvantage, to emerge and inspire the world through his story.

Final Thoughts

You have so much to live for. Your life is valuable, and you are needed in this world. People are depending on you to emerge so they can see that there is hope on the other side. You are the answer that they are looking for.

God has already given you everything you need to win in life. Everything you have been searching for is right within your reach. You must believe and lay hold of the treasure that God has uniquely placed on the inside of you.

Get excited about the future, embrace new beginnings, silence doubt, conquer your fears, forgive easily, love always, take huge risks, learn how to say no, master your plan, laugh a lot, release control, and only believe. Now spread your wings, emerge, and breakthrough into your destiny.

References

Relationship Study
http://consumer.healthday.com/encyclopedia/emotional-health-17/psychology-and-mental-health-news-566/health-benefits-of-friendship-648397.html

A Woman's Guide to Spiritual Warfare by Quinn Sherrer & Ruthanne Garlock

Nick Vujicic's Bio
https://en.wikipedia.org/wiki/Nick_Vujicic

About The Author

Fearlessly blazing her own trail, Chance Cessna is a renowned speaker, tv host, producer, author, ordained minister, and serial entrepreneur from Chicago, IL. Praised and respected as "the voice" of this next generation, Chance has graced the TEDx stage and has been featured on ABC, TV One, Essence, NBC, Lifetime, BET, and much more. Known for her warm and radiant personality, Chance's life motto is "Only Believe." On her free time, she loves to travel, dance, cook, and serve in her community.

Learn more about Chance at www.chancecessna.com.

SHARE YOUR EMERGE STORY WITH CHANCE!

Do you have a story about when you overcame the odds and came out on top? Chance wants to hear it! Submit your stories to emergethebook@gmail.com.

CONNECT WITH CHANCE ONLINE!

For more information on how to purchase bulk orders, shop for merchandise and/or book Chance for speaking engagements, visit www.chancecessna.com. We also invite you to leave a positive review online if you enjoyed this book!

Made in the USA
Columbia, SC
19 September 2019